# Recipe Collection

D1616219

Publications International, Ltd.

Favorite Brand Name Recipes at www.fbnr.com

**Pictured on the front cover (**top): Two-Tone Cheesecake Bars *(page 74);* (bottom, left to right): Raspberry-Topped Lemon Pie *(page 20),* Festive Fudge *(page 36),* and Cut-Out Cookies *(page 88).*

**Pictured on the back cover** (clockwise from bottom left): Ambrosia Freeze *(page 133),* Chilled Café Latte *(page 56),* Creamy Almond Candy *(page 47),* and German Chocolate Cake *(page 21).*

ISBN-13: 978-1-4127-2972-7
ISBN-10: 1-4127-2972-6

Library of Congress Control Number: 2008937304

Manufactured in China.

8 7 6 5 4 3 2 1

**Microwave Cooking:** Microwave ovens vary in wattage. Use the cooking times as guidelines and check for doneness before adding more time.

# CONTENTS

124

36

68

105

# CAKES & PIES

## Banana Pudding Cream Pie

1½ cups vanilla wafer crumbs (about 36 wafers)

⅓ cup butter or margarine, melted

¼ cup granulated sugar

1 (14-ounce) can **EAGLE BRAND®** Sweetened Condensed Milk (NOT evaporated milk)

4 egg yolks

½ cup water

1 (4-serving size) package cook-and-serve vanilla pudding and pie filling mix

1 (8-ounce) container sour cream, at room temperature

2 medium bananas, sliced, dipped in lemon juice and drained

Whipped cream

Additional banana slices, dipped in lemon juice and drained

Additional vanilla wafers

**1.** Preheat oven to 375°F. Combine wafer crumbs, butter and sugar; press firmly on bottom and up side to rim of 9-inch pie plate to form crust. Bake 8 to 10 minutes. Cool.

**2.** In heavy saucepan, combine **EAGLE BRAND®**, egg yolks, water and pudding mix; stir until well blended. Over medium heat, cook and stir until thickened and bubbly. Cool 15 minutes. Beat in sour cream.

**3.** Arrange banana slices on bottom of baked crust. Pour filling over bananas; cover. Chill. Top with whipped cream. Garnish with additional banana slices and vanilla wafers. Store leftovers covered in refrigerator.

# STRAWBERRY CREAM CHEESE SHORTCAKE

2 cups biscuit baking mix

2 tablespoons granulated sugar

½ cup (1 stick) butter or margarine, softened

⅓ cup warm water

1 (8-ounce) package cream cheese, softened

1 (14-ounce) can **EAGLE BRAND®** Sweetened Condensed Milk (NOT evaporated milk)

⅓ cup lemon juice

1 teaspoon vanilla extract

1 quart (about 1½ pounds) fresh strawberries, cleaned, hulled and sliced

1 (13.5- or 16-ounce) package prepared strawberry glaze, chilled

Whipped topping or whipped cream

**1.** Preheat oven to 400°F. Lightly grease 9-inch square baking pan. In small bowl, combine biscuit mix and sugar. Add butter and water; beat until well blended.

**2.** Turn into prepared pan; with floured hands or spoon, press evenly over bottom. Bake 10 to 12 minutes or until toothpick inserted near center comes out clean. Cool.

**3.** In large bowl, beat cream cheese until fluffy. Gradually beat in **EAGLE BRAND®** until smooth. Stir in lemon juice and vanilla. Spread evenly over shortcake layer. Chill at least 3 hours or until set. Cut into squares.

**4.** In bowl, combine strawberries and glaze. Spoon over shortcake just before serving. Garnish with whipped topping. Store leftovers covered in refrigerator.

# Traditional Peanut Butter Pie

⅓ cup creamy peanut butter

¾ cup confectioners' sugar

1 (9-inch) baked pie crust

1 (14-ounce) can **EAGLE BRAND®** Sweetened Condensed Milk (NOT evaporated milk)

4 eggs, separated

½ cup water

1 (4-serving size) package cook-and-serve vanilla pudding and pie filling mix

1 (8-ounce) container sour cream, at room temperature

¼ teaspoon cream of tartar

6 tablespoons granulated sugar

**1.** Preheat oven to 350°F. In small bowl, cut peanut butter into confectioners' sugar until crumbly; sprinkle into crust.

**2.** In large saucepan, combine **EAGLE BRAND®**, egg yolks, water and pudding mix; cook and stir until thickened. Cool slightly; stir in sour cream. Pour into crust.

**3.** In small bowl, beat egg whites and cream of tartar with electric mixer on high speed until soft peaks form. Gradually beat in granulated sugar at medium speed, 1 tablespoon at a time; beat 4 minutes longer or until sugar is dissolved and stiff glossy peaks form.

**4.** Spread meringue over pie, carefully sealing to edge of crust to prevent meringue from shrinking. Bake 15 minutes or until golden. Cool 1 hour. Chill at least 3 hours. Store leftovers covered in refrigerator.

**TIP:** Egg whites reach the fullest volume if they are allowed to stand at room temperature for 30 minutes before beating. Egg whites must be completely free of egg yolk. Separate eggs while they are cold because the yolk is firm and less likely to break. To remove any traces of yolk, use a cotton swab or the corner of a paper towel. Always check that the bowl and beaters are clean and dry. The smallest trace of yolk, fat or water can prevent the whites from reaching maximum volume. Do not use plastic bowls, because they may have an oily film even after repeated washings.

# CRANBERRY CRUMB PIE

1   (9-inch) unbaked pie crust

1   (8-ounce) package cream
    cheese, softened

1   (14-ounce) can **EAGLE BRAND**®
    Sweetened Condensed Milk
    (NOT evaporated milk)

¼   cup lemon juice

3   tablespoons firmly packed
    light brown sugar, divided

2   tablespoons cornstarch

1   (16-ounce) can whole-berry
    cranberry sauce

¼   cup (½ stick) cold butter
    or margarine

⅓   cup all-purpose flour

¾   cup chopped walnuts

**1.** Preheat oven to 425°F. Bake pie crust 6 minutes; remove from oven. Reduce oven temperature to 375°F.

**2.** In large bowl, beat cream cheese until fluffy. Gradually beat in **EAGLE BRAND**® until smooth. Add lemon juice; mix well. Pour into baked crust.

**3.** In small bowl, combine 1 tablespoon brown sugar and cornstarch; mix well. Stir in cranberry sauce. Spoon evenly over cheese mixture.

**4.** In medium bowl, cut butter into flour and remaining 2 tablespoons brown sugar until crumbly. Stir in walnuts. Sprinkle evenly over cranberry mixture. Bake 45 to 50 minutes or until bubbly and golden. Cool. Serve at room temperature or chill. Store leftovers covered in refrigerator.

**TIP:** To bake a pie crust without the filling (called "blind baking"), prick the dough all over with a fork. Line the crust with aluminum foil, waxed paper, or parchment paper, and spread dried beans (or peas) or pie weights over the bottom. Weighing down the pie crust prevents it from puffing and losing its shape during baking. (After baking, the dried beans are not edible, but you can save them and reuse them for blind baking additional pie crusts.) Cool the pie crust completely before adding the filling.

# FUDGE RIBBON CAKE

1 (18.25- or 18.5-ounce) package chocolate cake mix

1 (8-ounce) package cream cheese, softened

2 tablespoons butter, softened

1 tablespoon cornstarch

1 (14-ounce) can **EAGLE BRAND®** Sweetened Condensed Milk (NOT evaporated milk)

1 egg

1 teaspoon vanilla extract

Confectioners' sugar

Chocolate Glaze (recipe follows, optional)

**1.** Preheat oven to 350°F. Grease and flour 13×9-inch baking pan. Prepare cake mix as package directs. Pour batter into prepared pan.

**2.** In small bowl, beat cream cheese, butter and cornstarch with electric mixer on low speed until fluffy. Stop and scrape sides of bowl. Gradually beat in **EAGLE BRAND®**, then egg and vanilla until smooth. Spoon evenly over cake batter.

**3.** Bake 40 to 45 minutes or until toothpick inserted near center comes out clean. Cool. Sprinkle with confectioners' sugar and drizzle with chocolate glaze (optional). Store leftovers covered in refrigerator.

**Serving suggestion:** Invert slices onto serving plate as shown; garnish as desired.

**Fudge Ribbon Bundt Cake:** Preheat oven to 350°F. Grease and flour 10-inch bundt pan. Prepare cake mix as package directs. Pour batter into prepared pan. Prepare cream cheese layer as directed above; spoon evenly over batter. Bake 50 to 55 minutes or until toothpick inserted near center comes out clean. Cool 10 minutes. Remove from pan. Cool. Prepare Chocolate Glaze and drizzle over cake. Store leftovers covered in refrigerator.

## CHOCOLATE GLAZE

2 (1-ounce) squares unsweetened or semisweet chocolate

2 tablespoons butter

½ cup sifted confectioners' sugar

⅓ cup whipping cream

½ teaspoon vanilla extract

**1.** In small saucepan, over low heat, melt chocolate and butter. Remove from heat.

**2.** Stir in confectioners' sugar, cream and vanilla. Return saucepan to heat and whisk until mixture is thick and glossy. Let cool to room temperature and drizzle over cooled cake.

# Banana Coconut Cream Pie

3 tablespoons cornstarch

1⅓ cups water

1 (14-ounce) can **EAGLE BRAND®** Sweetened Condensed Milk (NOT evaporated milk)

3 egg yolks, beaten

2 tablespoons butter or margarine

1 teaspoon vanilla extract

½ cup flaked coconut, toasted

2 medium bananas

2 tablespoons lemon juice

1 (9-inch) prepared graham cracker or baked pie crust

Whipped cream (optional)

Additional toasted coconut for garnish (optional)

**1.** In heavy saucepan over medium heat, dissolve cornstarch in water; stir in **EAGLE BRAND®** and egg yolks. Cook and stir until thickened and bubbly. Remove from heat; add butter and vanilla. Cool slightly. Fold in coconut; set aside.

**2.** Peel and slice bananas into ¼-inch-thick rounds. Toss banana slices gently with lemon juice; drain. Arrange bananas on bottom of crust. Pour filling over bananas.

**3.** Cover; refrigerate 4 hours or until set. Top with whipped cream (optional) and additional toasted coconut (optional). Store leftovers covered in refrigerator.

> **TIP:** To prepare toasted coconut in the microwave, evenly spread 1 cup of coconut on a microwavable plate. Heat on HIGH (100% power) 4 to 5 minutes or just until golden. Stir coconut after each minute of cooking to ensure even toasting. To toast coconut on the range-top, use a heavy-bottomed skillet. Cook over medium heat 2 to 3 minutes, stirring frequently, until the coconut is lightly browned. Remove from the skillet immediately. Cool before using.

# PERFECT PUMPKIN PIE

*Makes one (9-inch) pie*

1 (15-ounce) can pumpkin (2 cups)

1 (14-ounce) can **EAGLE BRAND®** Sweetened Condensed Milk (NOT evaporated milk)

2 eggs

1 teaspoon ground cinnamon

½ teaspoon ground ginger

½ teaspoon ground nutmeg

½ teaspoon salt

1 (9-inch) unbaked pie crust

Optional toppings (recipes follow)

**1.** Preheat oven to 425°F. In medium bowl, whisk pumpkin, **EAGLE BRAND®**, eggs, cinnamon, ginger, nutmeg and salt until smooth.

**2.** Pour into crust. Bake 15 minutes. Reduce oven temperature to 350°F and continue baking 35 to 40 minutes longer or until knife inserted 1 inch from crust comes out clean. Cool. Garnish as desired. Store leftovers covered in refrigerator.

## SOUR CREAM TOPPING

1½ cups sour cream

2 tablespoons granulated sugar

1 teaspoon vanilla extract

In medium bowl, combine sour cream, sugar and vanilla. After pie has baked 30 minutes at 350°F, spread mixture evenly over top; bake 10 minutes longer.

## STREUSEL TOPPING

½ cup firmly packed brown sugar

½ cup all-purpose flour

¼ cup (½ stick) cold butter or margarine

¼ cup chopped nuts

In medium bowl, combine brown sugar and flour. Cut in butter until crumbly. Stir in nuts. After pie has baked 30 minutes at 350°F, sprinkle streusel evenly over top; bake 10 minutes longer.

## CHOCOLATE GLAZE

½ cup semisweet chocolate chips

1 teaspoon shortening

In small saucepan over low heat, melt chocolate chips and shortening. Drizzle or spread over top of baked pie.

# PEACH CREAM CAKE

1  (10.75-ounce) loaf angel
   food cake, frozen

1  (14-ounce) can **EAGLE BRAND®**
   Sweetened Condensed Milk
   (NOT evaporated milk)

1  cup cold water

1  teaspoon almond extract

1  (4-serving size) package
   instant vanilla pudding
   and pie filling mix

2  cups (1 pint) whipping
   cream, whipped

4  cups sliced peeled fresh
   peaches (about 2 pounds)

**1.** Cut cake into ¼-inch slices; arrange half of slices on bottom of ungreased 13×9-inch baking dish.

**2.** In large bowl, combine **EAGLE BRAND®**, water and almond extract. Add pudding mix; beat well. Chill 5 minutes.

**3.** Fold in whipped cream. Spread half of cream mixture over cake slices; arrange half of peach slices on top. Top with remaining cake slices, cream filling and peach slices.

**4.** Chill 4 hours or until set. Cut into squares to serve. Store leftovers covered in refrigerator.

**TIP:** To peel a large quantity of peaches, first blanch them in boiling water about 30 seconds. Remove the peaches from the water with a slotted spoon and plunge them into cold water. You will able to easily pull off the skins with a paring knife. Please note that cut peaches turn brown quickly when exposed to air. To retard the browning, dip the cut surfaces in lemon or orange juice or a mixture of water and lemon juice (6 parts water to 1 part lemon juice).

# Raspberry-Topped Lemon Pie

3  egg yolks

1  (14-ounce) can **EAGLE BRAND®** Sweetened Condensed Milk (NOT evaporated milk)

½  cup lemon juice

1  (6-ounce) prepared graham cracker pie crust

1  (10- or 12-ounce) package frozen raspberries, thawed

1  tablespoon cornstarch

   Whipped topping

**1.** Preheat oven to 325°F. In large bowl, with mixer, beat egg yolks and **EAGLE BRAND®** until well blended. Stir in lemon juice. Pour into crust. Bake 30 minutes.

**2.** In saucepan, combine raspberries and cornstarch; cook and stir until mixture thickens and is clear. Spoon on top of pie. Chill at least 4 hours.

**3.** Top with whipped topping. Garnish as desired. Store leftovers covered in refrigerator.

# German Chocolate Cake

1  (18.25- or 18.5-ounce) package German chocolate cake mix

1  cup water

3  eggs

½  cup vegetable oil

1  (14-ounce) can **EAGLE BRAND®** Sweetened Condensed Milk (NOT evaporated milk), divided

3  tablespoons butter or margarine

1  egg yolk

⅓  cup chopped pecans

⅓  cup flaked coconut

1  teaspoon vanilla extract

**1.** Preheat oven to 350°F. Grease and flour 13×9-inch baking pan.

**2.** In large bowl, combine cake mix, water, 3 eggs, oil and ⅓ cup **EAGLE BRAND®**. Beat on low speed until moistened, then beat on high speed 2 minutes. Pour batter into prepared pan. Bake 40 to 45 minutes or until toothpick inserted near center comes out clean.

**3.** In small saucepan over low heat, combine remaining **EAGLE BRAND®**, butter and egg yolk. Cook and stir until thickened, about 6 minutes. Add pecans, coconut and vanilla; spread over warm cake. Store leftovers covered in refrigerator.

# Coconut Lemon Torte

*Makes one (9-inch) cake*

1 (14-ounce) can **EAGLE BRAND®** Sweetened Condensed Milk (NOT evaporated milk)

2 egg yolks

½ cup lemon juice

1 teaspoon grated lemon rind (optional)

Yellow food coloring (optional)

1 (18.25- or 18.5-ounce) package white cake mix

1 (4-ounce) container frozen nondairy whipped topping, thawed (about 1¾ cups)

Flaked coconut

**1.** In medium saucepan, combine **EAGLE BRAND®**, egg yolks, lemon juice, lemon rind (optional) and food coloring (optional). Over medium heat, cook and stir until slightly thickened, about 10 minutes. Chill.

**2.** Preheat oven to 350°F. Grease and flour two 9-inch round layer cake pans. Prepare cake mix as package directs. Pour batter into prepared pans. Bake 30 minutes or until toothpick inserted near centers comes out clean. Remove from pans. Cool.

**3.** With sharp knife, remove crust from top of each cake layer. Split layers. Spread equal portions of lemon mixture between layers and on top to within 1 inch of edge.

**4.** Frost side and 1-inch rim on top of cake with whipped topping. Coat side of cake with coconut; garnish as desired. Store leftovers covered in refrigerator.

# CREAMY LEMON PIE

- 3   egg yolks
- 1   (14-ounce) can **EAGLE BRAND®** Sweetened Condensed Milk (NOT evaporated milk)
- ½   cup lemon juice
- 1   (8- or 9-inch) prepared graham cracker or baked pie crust
- Whipped topping or whipped cream
- Lemon curl or grated lemon rind (optional)

**1.** Preheat oven to 325°F. Beat egg yolks in medium bowl; gradually beat in **EAGLE BRAND®** and lemon juice.

**2.** Pour into crust. Bake 30 to 35 minutes or until set. Remove from oven. Cool 1 hour. Chill at least 3 hours.

**3.** Before serving, spread whipped topping over pie. Garnish with lemon curl or rind (optional). Store leftovers covered in refrigerator.

**TIP:** To make a lemon curl, cut a strip of lemon rind—yellow part only; the white pith underneath the yellow rind has a bitter flavor—using a paring knife or lemon zester. Wind around a straw or chopstick, and secure with plastic wrap. Let stand 1 hour. To use, unwrap, slide the curl off the straw, and arrange attractively.

# SWEET POTATO PIE

1 pound sweet potatoes,*
  boiled and peeled

¼ cup (½ stick) butter
  or margarine

1 (14-ounce) can **EAGLE BRAND®**
  Sweetened Condensed Milk
  (NOT evaporated milk)

2 eggs

1 teaspoon grated orange rind

1 teaspoon vanilla extract

1 teaspoon ground cinnamon

1 teaspoon ground nutmeg

¼ teaspoon salt

1 (9-inch) unbaked pie crust

*For best results, use fresh sweet potatoes.*

**1.** Preheat oven to 350°F. In large bowl, beat sweet potatoes and butter until smooth. Add **EAGLE BRAND®**, eggs, orange rind, vanilla, cinnamon, nutmeg and salt; mix well.

**2.** Pour into crust. Bake 40 minutes or until golden brown. Cool. Garnish as desired. Store leftovers covered in refrigerator.

# KEY LIME PIE

3 eggs, separated

1 (14-ounce) can **EAGLE BRAND**® Sweetened Condensed Milk (NOT evaporated milk)

½ cup key lime juice

2 to 3 drops green food coloring (optional)

1 (9-inch) unbaked pie crust

¼ teaspoon cream of tartar

⅓ cup granulated sugar

**1.** Preheat oven to 325°F. In medium bowl, beat egg yolks; gradually beat in **EAGLE BRAND**® and lime juice. Stir in food coloring (optional). Pour into pie crust. Bake 30 minutes. Remove from oven. Increase oven temperature to 350°F.

**2.** In large bowl, beat egg whites and cream of tartar with electric mixer on high speed until soft peaks form. Gradually beat in sugar on medium speed, 1 tablespoon at a time; beat 4 minutes longer or until sugar is dissolved and stiff glossy peaks form.

**3.** Immediately spread meringue over hot pie, carefully sealing to edge of crust to prevent meringue from shrinking. Bake 15 minutes or until golden. Cool 1 hour. Chill at least 3 hours. Store leftovers covered in refrigerator.

> **TIP:** The green limes that are familiar to most of us are known as Persian limes and are grown in Florida, California and Mexico. However, Florida also produces another variety known as the key lime—a small, round yellow lime that is thought to have much more flavor than Persian limes. If you can't find fresh key limes or bottled key lime juice in a gourmet market, you can substitute fresh juice from Persian limes.

# Decadent Brownie Pie

1   (9-inch) unbaked pie crust

1   cup (6 ounces) semisweet
      chocolate chips

¼   cup (½ stick) butter
      or margarine

1   (14-ounce) can **EAGLE BRAND®**
      Sweetened Condensed Milk
      (NOT evaporated milk)

½   cup biscuit baking mix

2   eggs

1   teaspoon vanilla extract

1   cup chopped nuts
      Vanilla ice cream (optional)

**1.** Preheat oven to 375°F. Bake pie crust 10 minutes; remove from oven. Reduce oven temperature to 325°F.

**2.** In small saucepan, over low heat, melt chocolate chips with butter.

**3.** In large bowl, beat chocolate mixture, **EAGLE BRAND®**, biscuit mix, eggs and vanilla until smooth. Stir in nuts. Pour into prepared pie crust.

**4.** Bake 40 to 45 minutes or until center is set. Cool at least 1 hour. Serve warm or at room temperature with ice cream (optional). Store leftovers covered in refrigerator.

> **TIP:** Glass or dark metal pie pans produce a crisp, golden brown crust, while shiny aluminum pans usually produce a paler crust. One advantage of a glass pie pan is the ability to check the color of the crust during baking. If necessary, you may use a strip of aluminum foil to shield the pie edges to prevent them from burning before the rest of the pie is done.

# FLUFFY PEANUT BUTTER PIE

*Makes one (9-inch) pie*

¼ cup (½ stick) butter
   or margarine

2 cups finely crushed crème-
   filled chocolate sandwich
   cookies (about 20 cookies)

1 (8-ounce) package cream
   cheese, softened

1 cup smooth or crunchy
   peanut butter

1 (14-ounce) can **EAGLE BRAND®**
   Sweetened Condensed Milk
   (NOT evaporated milk)

3 tablespoons lemon juice

1 teaspoon vanilla extract

1 cup (½ pint) whipping
   cream, whipped

**1.** In small saucepan, over low heat, melt butter; stir in cookie crumbs. Press crumb mixture firmly on bottom and up side to rim of 9-inch pie plate; chill while preparing filling.

**2.** In large bowl, beat cream cheese until fluffy; add peanut butter and **EAGLE BRAND®**, beating until smooth. Stir in lemon juice and vanilla; fold in whipped cream.

**3.** Pour into crust. Chill 4 hours or until set. Garnish as desired. Store leftovers covered in refrigerator.

**TIP:** You can crush sandwich cookies quickly, easily and with no mess. Place them in a resealable plastic food storage bag, seal the bag, then run a rolling pin over the bag several times to pulverize the cookies. Shake the bag as needed and repeat the rolling until all the cookies have become fine crumbs.

# Holiday Mini Cherry Pound Cakes

*Makes 6 mini loaves*

1¼ cups (2½ sticks) butter or
   margarine, softened

2¾ cups granulated sugar

5 eggs

1 teaspoon vanilla extract

3 cups all-purpose flour

1 teaspoon baking powder

¼ teaspoon salt

1 (14-ounce) can **EAGLE BRAND®**
   Sweetened Condensed Milk
   (NOT evaporated milk)

2 cups quartered maraschino
   cherries, well drained

**1.** Preheat oven to 350°F. Grease and flour 6 mini loaf pans.

**2.** In large bowl, beat butter, sugar, eggs and vanilla with electric mixer on low speed until blended, then on high speed 5 minutes until light and fluffy.

**3.** Combine flour, baking powder and salt. Add flour mixture alternately with **EAGLE BRAND®** to creamed mixture, mixing lightly after each addition. Fold in cherries. Turn batter evenly into prepared pans.

**4.** Bake 45 minutes or until light brown. Let cool in pan 5 minutes; invert loaves onto rack and let cool completely. Store leftovers covered.

**TIP:** Create delicious homemade gifts by baking cakes in decorative aluminum loaf pans and wrapping with a festive bow.

# BERRY BERRY COOL PIE

1 (14-ounce) can **EAGLE BRAND**®
Sweetened Condensed Milk
(NOT evaporated milk)

½ cup lemon juice

1½ to 2 cups assorted fresh
berries (raspberries,
blueberries or blackberries)

1 (8-ounce) container frozen
nondairy whipped
topping, thawed

1 (6-ounce) prepared graham
cracker pie crust

**1.** In large bowl, mix together **EAGLE BRAND**® and lemon juice; combine well.
Mix in berries. Fold in whipped topping. Spoon mixture into crust.

**2.** Freeze 5 hours or until set. Let stand 30 to 40 minutes before serving. Garnish
as desired. Store leftovers covered in freezer.

# Chocolate Truffle Pie

1 envelope unflavored gelatin

½ cup water

3 (1-ounce) squares unsweetened or semisweet chocolate, melted and cooled

1 (14-ounce) can **EAGLE BRAND®** Sweetened Condensed Milk (NOT evaporated milk)

1 teaspoon vanilla extract

2 cups (1 pint) whipping cream, whipped

1 (6-ounce) prepared chocolate crumb pie crust

**1.** In small saucepan, sprinkle gelatin over water; let stand 1 minute. Over low heat, stir until gelatin dissolves.

**2.** In large bowl, beat chocolate and **EAGLE BRAND®** until smooth. Stir in gelatin mixture and vanilla. Fold in whipped cream. Pour into prepared crust.

**3.** Chill 3 hours or until set. Garnish as desired. Store leftovers covered in refrigerator.

# APPLE SPICE CUSTARD CAKE

1 (18.25-ounce) package spice cake mix

2 medium apples, peeled, cored and chopped

1 (14-ounce) can **EAGLE BRAND®** Sweetened Condensed Milk (NOT evaporated milk)

1 (8-ounce) container sour cream

¼ cup lemon juice

Ground cinnamon (optional)

**1.** Preheat oven to 350°F. Grease and flour 13×9-inch baking pan. Prepare cake mix according to package directions.

**2.** Stir in apples. Pour batter into prepared pan. Bake 30 to 35 minutes or until toothpick inserted near center comes out clean.

**3.** In medium bowl, combine **EAGLE BRAND®** and sour cream; mix well. Stir in lemon juice. Remove cake from oven; spread sour cream mixture evenly over hot cake.

**4.** Return to oven; bake 5 minutes or until set. Sprinkle with cinnamon (optional). Cool. Chill. Store leftovers covered in refrigerator.

# Chocolate Chiffon Pie

2  (1-ounce) squares unsweetened chocolate, chopped

1  (14-ounce) can **EAGLE BRAND®** Sweetened Condensed Milk (NOT evaporated milk)

1  envelope unflavored gelatin

⅓  cup water

½  teaspoon vanilla extract

1  cup (½ pint) whipping cream, whipped

1  (6-ounce) prepared chocolate or graham cracker pie crust

Additional whipped cream

Shaved chocolate (optional)

**1.** In medium-heavy saucepan over low heat, melt chocolate with **EAGLE BRAND®**.

**2.** In small saucepan, sprinkle gelatin over water; let stand 1 minute. Over low heat, stir until gelatin dissolves.

**3.** Combine chocolate mixture and gelatin. Add vanilla. Cool to room temperature. Fold in whipped cream. Spread into crust.

**4.** Chill 3 hours or until set. Garnish with additional whipped cream and shaved chocolate (optional). Store leftovers covered in refrigerator.

# Lemon Icebox Pie

1 (14-ounce) can **EAGLE BRAND**® Sweetened Condensed Milk (NOT evaporated milk)

½ cup lemon juice

Yellow food coloring (optional)

1 cup (½ pint) whipping cream, whipped

1 (6-ounce) prepared graham cracker or baked pie crust

**1.** In medium bowl, combine **EAGLE BRAND**®, lemon juice and food coloring (optional). Fold in whipped cream.

**2.** Pour into crust. Chill 3 hours or until set. Garnish as desired. Store leftovers covered in refrigerator.

# CHOCOLATE MOUSSE CAKE

1 (18.25- or 18.5-ounce) package chocolate cake mix

1 (14-ounce) can **EAGLE BRAND®** Sweetened Condensed Milk (NOT evaporated milk)

2 (1-ounce) squares unsweetened chocolate, melted

½ cup cold water

1 (4-serving size) package instant chocolate pudding and pie filling mix

1 cup (½ pint) whipping cream, stiffly whipped

**1.** Preheat oven to 350°F. Grease and flour two 9-inch round layer cake pans. Prepare and bake cake mix as package directs. Remove cakes from pans. Cool.

**2.** In large bowl, beat **EAGLE BRAND®** and chocolate until well blended. Gradually beat in water and pudding mix until smooth. Chill 30 minutes. Beat until smooth. Fold in whipped cream. Chill at least 1 hour.

**3.** Place cake layer on serving plate; top with 1½ cups mousse mixture. Top with remaining cake layer. Frost side and top of cake with remaining mousse.

# MAGIC QUICK CHOCOLATE FROSTING

1 (14-ounce) can **EAGLE BRAND®** Sweetened Condensed Milk (NOT evaporated milk)

2 (1-ounce) squares unsweetened or semisweet chocolate

⅛ teaspoon salt

3 tablespoons water

1 teaspoon vanilla extract

**1.** In heavy saucepan, over medium heat, combine **EAGLE BRAND®**, chocolate and salt. Cook and stir rapidly until chocolate melts and mixture thickens, about 8 minutes.

**2.** Remove from heat; stir in water and vanilla. Cook and stir rapidly until thickened again, about 4 minutes. Cool 10 minutes. Store at room temperature. Frosts 1 (8- or 9-inch) 2-layer or 1 (13×9-inch) cake or 2 dozen cupcakes.

# Surprise-in-a-Pocket Cupcakes

3  eggs, divided

2  (3-ounce) packages cream cheese, softened

1  (14-ounce) can **EAGLE BRAND®** Sweetened Condensed Milk (NOT evaporated milk), divided

1  (18.25- or 18.5-ounce) package chocolate cake mix

1⅓  cups water

   Chocolate Frosting *(recipe follows)*

**1.** Preheat oven to 375°F. Place paper liners in 36 (2½-inch) muffin cups. Separate 1 egg yolk from white. In large bowl, beat cream cheese until fluffy. Gradually beat in ⅓ cup **EAGLE BRAND®** and egg yolk; set aside.

**2.** In large bowl, combine cake mix, remaining **EAGLE BRAND®**, water, 2 eggs and egg white. Beat with electric mixer on low speed until moistened; beat on high speed 2 minutes.

**3.** Divide batter among prepared muffin cups, filling each ⅔ full. Add rounded teaspoonful of cream cheese mixture to center of each muffin tin.

**4.** Bake 18 minutes or until tops spring back when lightly touched. (Filling will sink during baking). Cool on wire rack.

**5.** Frost cupcakes with Chocolate Frosting (about 2 tablespoons each). If desired, decorate one at a time (do not wait until end to decorate, as top of frosting sets quickly). Store leftovers at room temperature.

## Chocolate Frosting

1  (14-ounce) can **EAGLE BRAND®** Sweetened Condensed Milk (NOT evaporated milk)

1  cup (6 ounces) semisweet chocolate chips

⅛  teaspoon salt

2  cups confectioners' sugar

1  teaspoon vanilla extract

**1.** In heavy medium-sized saucepan, combine **EAGLE BRAND®**, chocolate chips and salt. Cook and stir over medium heat until chips melt; cook and stir 3 minutes longer. Remove from heat; cool 15 minutes.

**2.** With mixer, beat in confectioners' sugar and vanilla until smooth.

*Makes about 4 cups frosting*

# CANDIES & BEVERAGES

## FESTIVE FUDGE

| | |
|---|---|
| 3 cups (18 ounces) semisweet or milk chocolate chips | ⅛ teaspoon salt |
| 1 (14-ounce) can **EAGLE BRAND®** Sweetened Condensed Milk (NOT evaporated milk) | ½ to 1 cup chopped nuts (optional) |
| | 1½ teaspoons vanilla extract |

**1.** Line 8- or 9-inch square pan with foil, extending foil over edges of pan. Butter foil; set aside.

**2.** In heavy saucepan over low heat, melt chocolate chips with **EAGLE BRAND®** and salt. Remove from heat; stir in nuts (optional) and vanilla. Spread evenly in prepared pan.

**3.** Chill 2 hours or until firm. Turn fudge onto cutting board; peel off foil and cut into squares. Store leftovers covered in refrigerator.

**Chocolate Peanut Butter Chip Glazed Fudge:** Proceed as above, but substitute ¾ cup peanut butter chips for nuts. For glaze, melt additional ½ cup peanut butter chips with ½ cup whipping cream; stir until thick and smooth. Spread over chilled fudge.

**Marshmallow Fudge:** Proceed as above, but add 2 tablespoons butter to chocolate mixture, and fold in 2 cups miniature marshmallows instead of nuts.

> **TIP:** Create delicious homemade gifts from an assortment of flavored fudges, packed in decorative tins, candy bags or boxes. Wrap individual pieces of fudge in colored food-grade cellophane, candy wrappers or gold or silver foil candy cups and arrange in gift bags or tins. Store in refrigerator.

# Homemade Irish Cream Liqueur

*Makes about 5 cups*

2 cups whipping cream
or coffee cream

1 (14-ounce) can **EAGLE BRAND®**
Sweetened Condensed Milk
(NOT evaporated milk)

1¼ to 1¾ cups Irish whiskey,
brandy, rum, bourbon,
Scotch or rye whiskey

2 tablespoons chocolate syrup

2 teaspoons instant coffee

1 teaspoon vanilla extract

½ teaspoon almond extract

**1.** In blender container, combine whipping cream, **EAGLE BRAND®**, whiskey, chocolate syrup, coffee, vanilla and almond extracts; blend until smooth.

**2.** Serve over ice. Store leftovers tightly covered in refrigerator.

**Homemade Cream Liqueur:** Omit Irish whiskey, chocolate syrup, coffee and extracts. Add 1¼ cups flavored liqueur (almond, coffee, orange or mint) to **EAGLE BRAND®** and cream. Proceed as directed above.

**TIP:** For a more blended flavor, store the homemade liqueur in the refrigerator for several hours before serving.

# Mocha Madness

*Makes 6 servings*

6 cups strong brewed coffee

¾ cup **EAGLE BRAND®** Sweetened
Condensed Milk (NOT
evaporated milk)

¾ cup chocolate syrup

Whipped cream (optional)

Chocolate shavings (optional)

**1.** In large saucepan, combine coffee, **EAGLE BRAND®** and chocolate syrup. Over low heat, cook and stir until coffee is hot.

**2.** Pour 1¼ cups coffee mixture into 12-ounce mugs. Garnish with whipped cream (optional) and chocolate shavings (optional). Serve immediately. Store leftovers covered in refrigerator.

*Homemade Irish Cream Liqueur*

# CHOCOLATE TRUFFLES

3 cups (18 ounces) semisweet chocolate chips

1 (14-ounce) can **EAGLE BRAND®** Sweetened Condensed Milk (NOT evaporated milk)

1 tablespoon vanilla extract

Coatings: finely chopped toasted nuts, flaked coconut, chocolate sprinkles, colored sugar, unsweetened cocoa, confectioners' sugar or colored sprinkles

**1.** In large saucepan over low heat, melt chocolate chips with **EAGLE BRAND®**. Remove from heat; stir in vanilla.

**2.** Pour into medium bowl, cover and chill 2 to 3 hours or until firm.

**3.** Shape into 1-inch balls; roll in desired coating. Chill 1 hour or until firm. Store leftovers covered in refrigerator.

**Microwave Directions:** In 1-quart glass measure, combine chocolate chips and **EAGLE BRAND®**. Microwave on HIGH (100% power) 3 minutes, stirring after 1½ minutes. Stir until smooth. Proceed as directed above.

**Amaretto Truffles:** Substitute 3 tablespoons amaretto liqueur and ½ teaspoon almond extract for vanilla. Roll in finely chopped toasted almonds.

**Orange Truffles:** Substitute 3 tablespoons orange-flavored liqueur for vanilla. Roll in finely chopped toasted almonds mixed with finely grated orange peel.

**Rum Truffles:** Substitute ¼ cup dark rum for vanilla. Roll in flaked coconut.

**Bourbon Truffles:** Substitute 3 tablespoons bourbon for vanilla. Roll in finely chopped toasted nuts.

# CRANBERRY CREAM PUNCH

Cranberry Ice Ring (recipe follows) or ice

1 (14-ounce) can **EAGLE BRAND®** Sweetened Condensed Milk (NOT evaporated milk)

1 (12-ounce) can frozen cranberry juice cocktail concentrate, thawed

1 cup cranberry-flavored liqueur (optional)

Red food coloring (optional)

2 (1-liter) bottles club soda or ginger ale, chilled

**1.** Prepare Cranberry Ice Ring one day in advance.

**2.** In punch bowl, combine **EAGLE BRAND®**, cranberry concentrate, liqueur (optional) and food coloring (optional).

**3.** Just before serving, add club soda and prepared Cranberry Ice Ring to punch bowl, or add ice cubes. Store leftovers covered in refrigerator.

## CRANBERRY ICE RING

2 cups cranberry juice cocktail

1½ cups water

¾ to 1 cup cranberries and lime slices or mint leaves

**1.** Combine cranberry juice cocktail and water in large bowl. Pour ½ cup cranberry liquid into 1½-quart ring mold. Arrange cranberries and lime slices or mint leaves in mold; freeze 2 hours.

**2.** Add remaining 3 cups cranberry liquid to mold; freeze overnight.

**3.** Unmold in warm water and float in punch bowl.

*Makes 1 ice ring*

# Peppermint Chocolate Fudge

*Makes about 2 pounds*

2 cups (12 ounces) milk chocolate chips

1 cup (6 ounces) semisweet chocolate chips

1 (14-ounce) can **EAGLE BRAND®** Sweetened Condensed Milk (NOT evaporated milk)

⅛ teaspoon salt

½ teaspoon peppermint extract

¾ cup crushed hard peppermint candy

**1.** Line 8- or 9-inch square pan with foil, extending foil over edges of pan. Butter foil; set aside.

**2.** In heavy saucepan over low heat, melt chocolate chips with **EAGLE BRAND®** and salt. Remove from heat; stir in peppermint extract. Spread evenly in prepared pan. Sprinkle with peppermint candy.

**3.** Chill 2 hours or until firm. Turn fudge onto cutting board; peel off foil and cut into squares. Store leftovers covered in refrigerator.

# Strawberry Bonbons

*Makes about 2½ pounds or about 4 dozen bonbons*

1 (14-ounce) can **EAGLE BRAND®** Sweetened Condensed Milk (NOT evaporated milk)

1 (14-ounce) package flaked coconut

1 cup ground blanched almonds

1 (6-ounce) package strawberry-flavored gelatin, divided

1 teaspoon almond extract

Red food coloring

2 cups sifted confectioners' sugar

½ cup whipping cream

Green food coloring

**1.** In large bowl, combine **EAGLE BRAND®**, coconut, almonds, ⅓ cup gelatin, almond extract and enough red food coloring to tint mixture to desired strawberry red shade. Transfer mixture to food processor and pulse several times to form paste. Chill until firm enough to handle.

**2.** Shape spoonfuls of coconut mixture (about ¾ tablespoon) into strawberry shapes. Sprinkle remaining gelatin on flat dish; roll each strawberry in gelatin to coat. Place on wax paper-lined baking sheet; chill.

**3.** To make frosting "hulls," combine confectioners' sugar, whipping cream and green food coloring until well blended. Fill pastry bag fitted with open star tip with frosting; pipe small amount on top of each strawberry to form hull. Store leftovers tightly covered in refrigerator.

**TIP:** You may also make these candies in other shapes and flavors. For example, make cherry bonbons by using cherry-flavored gelatin, and add black licorice candy stems. Just match the food color you use to tint the mixture to the flavor and color of the gelatin you use, then use edible garnishes for any stems you want to add.

# ROCKY ROAD CANDY

*Makes about 3½ dozen candies*

2 cups (12 ounces) semisweet chocolate chips

1 (14-ounce) can **EAGLE BRAND®** Sweetened Condensed Milk (NOT evaporated milk)

2 tablespoons butter or margarine

2 cups dry-roasted peanuts

1 (10½-ounce) package miniature marshmallows

**1.** Line 13×9-inch baking pan with foil, extending foil over edges of pan. Butter foil; set aside.

**2.** In large heavy saucepan over low heat, melt chocolate chips with **EAGLE BRAND®** and butter. Remove from heat.

**3.** In large bowl, combine peanuts and marshmallows; stir in chocolate mixture. Spread evenly in prepared pan.

**4.** Chill 2 hours or until firm. Remove candy from pan; peel off foil and cut into squares. Store leftovers loosely covered at room temperature.

**Microwave Method:** In 1-quart glass measure, combine chocolate chips, **EAGLE BRAND®** and butter. Microwave on HIGH (100% power) 3 minutes, stirring after 1½ minutes. Let stand 5 minutes. Proceed as directed above

# CREAMY ALMOND CANDY

*Makes about 3¼ pounds*

1½ pounds vanilla-flavored candy coating*

1 (14-ounce) can **EAGLE BRAND®** Sweetened Condensed Milk (NOT evaporated milk)

⅛ teaspoon salt

3 cups (about 1 pound) whole almonds, toasted**

1 teaspoon almond extract

*Also called confectioners' coating.

**To toast almonds, spread in single layer in heavy-bottomed skillet. Cook over medium heat 2 to 3 minutes, stirring frequently, until nuts are lightly browned. Remove from skillet immediately. Cool before using.

**1.** Line 15×10-inch jelly roll pan with wax paper; set aside.

**2.** In heavy saucepan over low heat, melt candy coating with **EAGLE BRAND®** and salt. Remove from heat; stir in almonds and almond extract. Spread evenly in prepared pan.

**3.** Chill 2 hours or until firm. Turn onto cutting board; peel off paper and cut into triangles or squares. Store leftovers tightly covered at room temperature.

**Microwave method:** In 2-quart glass measure, combine candy coating, **EAGLE BRAND®** and salt. Microwave on HIGH (100% power) 3 to 5 minutes, stirring after each 1½ minutes. Stir until smooth. Proceed as directed above.

# Chocolate Snow Swirl Fudge

*Makes about 2 pounds*

3 cups (18 ounces) semisweet chocolate chips

1 (14-ounce) can **EAGLE BRAND®** Sweetened Condensed Milk (NOT evaporated milk)

¼ cup (½ stick) butter or margarine, divided

⅛ teaspoon salt

1 cup chopped nuts

1½ teaspoons vanilla extract

2 cups miniature marshmallows

**1.** Line 8- or 9-inch square pan with foil, extending foil over edges of pan. Butter foil; set aside.

**2.** In large heavy saucepan over low heat, melt chocolate chips with **EAGLE BRAND®**, 2 tablespoons butter and salt. Remove from heat; stir in nuts and vanilla. Spread evenly in prepared pan.

**3.** In small saucepan over low heat, melt marshmallows with remaining 2 tablespoons butter; stir until smooth. Spread on top of fudge. With knife or metal spatula, swirl through fudge to marble.

**4.** Chill 2 hours or until firm. Turn fudge onto cutting board; peel off foil and cut into squares. Store leftovers covered in refrigerator.

# CREAMY HOT CHOCOLATE

*Makes about 8 cups*

1 (14-ounce) can **EAGLE BRAND®** Sweetened Condensed Milk (NOT evaporated milk)

½ cup unsweetened cocoa powder

1½ teaspoons vanilla extract

⅛ teaspoon salt

6½ cups hot water

Miniature marshmallows (optional)

**1.** In large saucepan over medium heat, combine **EAGLE BRAND®**, cocoa, vanilla and salt; mix well.

**2.** Slowly stir in water. Heat through, stirring occasionally. Do not boil. Top with marshmallows (optional). Store leftovers covered in refrigerator.

**Microwave Method:** In 2-quart glass measure, combine all ingredients except marshmallows. Microwave on HIGH (100% power) 8 to 10 minutes, stirring every 3 minutes. Top with marshmallows (optional).

**TIP:** Leftover Creamy Hot Chocolate can be stored in refrigerator up to 5 days. Mix well and reheat before serving.

# CANDY CRUNCH

*Makes about 1¾ pounds*

4 cups (half of 15-ounce bag) pretzel sticks or pretzel twists

4 cups (24 ounces) white chocolate chips

1 (14-ounce) can **EAGLE BRAND®** Sweetened Condensed Milk (NOT evaporated milk)

1 cup dried fruit (dried cranberries, raisins or mixed dried fruit bits)

**1.** Line 15×10-inch jelly roll pan with foil. Place pretzels in large bowl.

**2.** In large saucepan over low heat, melt white chocolate chips with **EAGLE BRAND®**. Cook and stir constantly until smooth. Pour over pretzels, stirring to coat.

**3.** Immediately spread mixture into prepared pan. Sprinkle with dried fruit; press down lightly with back of spoon. Chill 1 to 2 hours or until set. Break into chunks. Store leftovers loosely covered at room temperature.

# CHOCOLATE AND BUTTERSCOTCH FUDGE

*Makes about 2 pounds*

2 cups (12 ounces) semisweet chocolate chips

1 (14-ounce) can **EAGLE BRAND®** Sweetened Condensed Milk (NOT evaporated milk), divided

½ cup chopped walnuts (optional)

1 teaspoon vanilla extract

1 cup butterscotch chips

**1.** Line 8- or 9-inch square pan with foil, extending foil over edges of pan. Butter foil; set aside.

**2.** In heavy saucepan over low heat, melt chocolate chips with 1 cup **EAGLE BRAND®**. Remove from heat; stir in nuts (optional) and vanilla. Spread evenly into prepared pan.

**3.** In clean heavy saucepan over low heat, melt butterscotch chips and remaining **EAGLE BRAND®**. Spread evenly over chocolate layer.

**4.** Chill 3 hours or until firm. Turn fudge onto cutting board; peel off foil and cut into squares. Store leftovers covered in refrigerator.

# White Christmas Jewel Fudge

*Makes 2¼ pounds*

3 cups (18 ounces) premium white chocolate chips

1 (14-ounce) can **EAGLE BRAND®** Sweetened Condensed Milk (NOT evaporated milk)

1½ teaspoons vanilla extract

⅛ teaspoon salt

½ cup chopped green candied cherries

½ cup chopped red candied cherries

**1.** Line 8- or 9-inch square pan with foil, extending foil over edges of pan. Butter foil; set aside.

**2.** In large heavy saucepan over low heat, melt white chocolate chips with **EAGLE BRAND®**, vanilla and salt. Remove from heat; stir in cherries. Spread evenly in prepared pan.

**3.** Chill 2 hours or until firm. Turn fudge onto cutting board; peel off foil and cut into squares. Store leftovers covered in refrigerator.

**Rum Raisin White Fudge:** Omit vanilla and cherries. Add 1½ teaspoons white vinegar, 1 teaspoon rum flavoring and ¾ cup raisins. Proceed as above.

**Toasted Nutty White Fudge:** Omit cherries. Add 1 cup chopped toasted nuts. Proceed as above.

# APPLE PIE SHAKE

1 (14-ounce) can **EAGLE BRAND®** Sweetened Condensed Milk (NOT evaporated milk), chilled

1 cup applesauce, chilled

½ cup apple juice or apple cider, chilled

½ teaspoon apple pie spice*

3 cups crushed ice

Apple wedges and apple peel strips (optional)

*Look for apple pie spice in the spice section of your supermarket, or substitute a mixture of ¼ teaspoon ground cinnamon, ⅛ teaspoon ground nutmeg and a dash of ground allspice.*

**1.** In blender container, combine **EAGLE BRAND®**, applesauce, apple juice and apple pie spice; cover and blend until smooth.

**2.** With blender running, gradually add ice, blending until smooth. Serve immediately. Garnish with apple wedges and apple peel strips (optional).

# COOKIES 'N CREAM FUDGE

3   (6-ounce) packages white
    chocolate baking squares

1   (14-ounce) can **EAGLE BRAND**®
    Sweetened Condensed Milk
    (NOT evaporated milk)

⅛   teaspoon salt

3   cups coarsely crushed chocolate
    crème-filled sandwich
    cookies (about 20 cookies)

**1.** Line 8- or 9-inch square pan with foil, extending foil over edges of pan. Butter foil; set aside.

**2.** In heavy saucepan over low heat, melt white chocolate squares, **EAGLE BRAND**® and salt. Remove from heat; stir in crushed cookies. Spread evenly in prepared pan.

**3.** Chill 2 hours or until firm. Turn fudge onto cutting board; peel off foil and cut into squares. Store leftovers covered in refrigerator.

**Variation:** Use any of your other favorite cookies, coarsely crushed to yield 3 cups. Proceed as above.

# CHOCOLATE SWIZZLE NOG

2 cups milk

1 (14-ounce) can **EAGLE BRAND®** Sweetened Condensed Milk (NOT evaporated milk)

2 tablespoons unsweetened cocoa

½ teaspoon vanilla or peppermint extract

Whipped cream or whipped topping

**1.** In medium saucepan over medium heat, combine milk, **EAGLE BRAND®** and cocoa. Heat through, stirring constantly. Remove from heat; stir in vanilla.

**2.** Serve warm in mugs topped with whipped cream. Store leftovers covered in refrigerator.

# CHILLED CAFÉ LATTE

2 tablespoons instant coffee

¾ cup warm water

1 (14-ounce) can **EAGLE BRAND®**
Fat Free or Original
Sweetened Condensed Milk
(NOT evaporated milk)

1 teaspoon vanilla extract

4 cups ice cubes

**1.** In blender container, dissolve coffee in water. Add **EAGLE BRAND®** and vanilla; cover and blend on high speed until smooth.

**2.** With blender running, gradually add ice cubes, blending until smooth. Serve immediately. Store leftovers covered in refrigerator.

# PEANUT BUTTER FUDGE

*Makes about 2¼ pounds*

1  (14-ounce) can **EAGLE BRAND®** Sweetened Condensed Milk (NOT evaporated milk)

½  cup creamy peanut butter

2  (6-ounce) packages white chocolate squares or white baking bars, chopped

¾  cup chopped peanuts

1  teaspoon vanilla extract

**1.** Line 8- or 9-inch square pan with foil, extending foil over edges of pan. Butter foil; set aside.

**2.** In heavy saucepan over medium heat, cook **EAGLE BRAND®** and peanut butter just until bubbly, stirring constantly. Remove from heat; stir in white chocolate until smooth. Immediately stir in peanuts and vanilla. Spread evenly in prepared pan.

**3.** Chill 2 hours or until firm. Turn fudge onto cutting board; peel off foil and cut into squares. Store leftovers covered in refrigerator.

# PARTY MINTS

1   (14-ounce) can **EAGLE BRAND®** Sweetened Condensed Milk (NOT evaporated milk)

5½  cups confectioners' sugar

½   teaspoon peppermint extract

Assorted colored granulated sugar or crystals

**1.** In medium bowl, beat **EAGLE BRAND®** and half of confectioners' sugar until blended. Gradually add remaining confectioners' sugar and peppermint extract, beating until stiff.

**2.** Shape mixture into ½-inch balls. Roll in colored sugar; place on parchment paper. Let stand 8 hours to set. Store covered at room temperature.

**Chocolate Party Mints:** Dip uncoated mints in melted bittersweet chocolate.

> **TIP:** You can color granulated or crystal sugar to match the decor for any occasion. Use liquid food color, and add it to the sugar a drop at a time; mix the sugar well until the color is evenly distributed. If you prefer a darker shade, add more color until the sugar reaches the desired color. You can also create your own custom colors by blending different food colors; use color charts as a guide.

# CAPPUCCINO CARAMELS ROYALE

*Makes about 3 pounds or 5 dozen caramels*

1 cup (2 sticks) butter

2 (1-ounce) squares unsweetened chocolate, chopped

2¼ cups firmly packed brown sugar

1 (14-ounce) can **EAGLE BRAND®** Sweetened Condensed Milk (NOT evaporated milk)

1 cup light corn syrup

1 tablespoon instant coffee crystals

1 cup chopped pecans or walnuts (optional)

**1.** Line 8-inch square pan with foil, extending foil over edges of pan. Butter foil; set aside.

**2.** In heavy 3-quart saucepan, melt 1 cup butter and chocolate. Stir in brown sugar, **EAGLE BRAND®**, corn syrup and coffee crystals. Clip candy thermometer to side of pan. Cook over medium heat, stirring constantly, until thermometer reads 248°F (firm-ball stage*). Mixture should boil at moderate, steady rate, bubbling evenly over entire surface, to reach firm-ball stage, about 15 to 20 minutes.

**3.** Remove from heat. Remove thermometer. Immediately stir in nuts (optional). Quickly pour into prepared pan, spreading evenly with spoon. Cool.

**4.** When candy is firm, use foil to lift candy out of pan. Use buttered knife to cut into squares. Wrap each square in plastic wrap or place in candy cups if desired.

*To test candy, spoon a few drops of the hot caramel into a cup of cold (but not icy) water. Use your fingers to form the drops into a ball. Remove the ball from the water. If it holds its shape but quickly flattens at room temperature, it has reached firm-ball stage. If the mixture hasn't reached the correct stage, continue cooking and re-test again with fresh cold water and a clean spoon.*

**TIP:** To ensure the best texture and results, butter—not margarine—should be used in most candy recipes. Butter also contributes a rich, creamy flavor to candies. Today, many margarines contain water, which is added to decrease the amount of fat per serving. Margarine-type products marked as "spreads" or those that come in tubs should *not* be used because the water content will cause melted chocolate to become stiff and grainy. Also, the added water will change the cooking times for cooked candies. If you must use margarine, use only *stick products labeled as margarine.*

# CHEESECAKES & SQUARES

## ALMOND PRALINE CHEESECAKE

*Makes one (9-inch) or (13×9-inch) cheesecake*

¾ cup graham cracker crumbs

½ cup slivered almonds, toasted and finely chopped

¼ cup firmly packed brown sugar

¼ cup (½ stick) butter or margarine, melted

3 (8-ounce) packages cream cheese, softened

1 (14-ounce) can **EAGLE BRAND®** Sweetened Condensed Milk (NOT evaporated milk)

3 eggs

1 teaspoon almond extract

Almond Praline Topping (recipe follows)

**1.** Preheat oven to 300°F. In medium bowl, combine graham cracker crumbs, almonds, brown sugar and butter; press on bottom of ungreased 9-inch springform pan or 13×9-inch baking pan.

**2.** In large bowl, beat cream cheese until fluffy. Gradually beat in **EAGLE BRAND®** until smooth. Add eggs and almond extract; mix well. Pour onto prepared crust.

**3.** Bake 55 to 60 minutes or until center is set. Cool. Top with Almond Praline Topping. Chill. Store leftovers covered in refrigerator.

### ALMOND PRALINE TOPPING

⅓ cup firmly packed dark brown sugar

⅓ cup whipping cream

½ cup slivered almonds, toasted and chopped

In small saucepan over medium heat, combine brown sugar and whipping cream. Cook and stir until sugar dissolves. Simmer 5 minutes or until thickened. Remove from heat; add almonds. Spoon evenly over cheesecake.

*Makes about 1 cup*

**Note:** To make topping for 13×9-inch cheesecake, double all topping ingredients; simmer 10 to 12 minutes or until thickened.

# CREAMY BAKED CHEESECAKE

1¼ cups graham cracker crumbs

⅓ cup butter or margarine, melted

¼ cup granulated sugar

2 (8-ounce) packages cream cheese, softened

1 (14-ounce) can **EAGLE BRAND®** Sweetened Condensed Milk (NOT evaporated milk)

3 eggs

¼ cup lemon juice

1 (8-ounce) container sour cream, at room temperature

Raspberry Topping (recipe follows, optional)

**1.** Preheat oven to 300°F. In small bowl, combine graham cracker crumbs, butter and sugar; press firmly on bottom of ungreased 9-inch springform pan.

**2.** In large bowl, beat cream cheese until fluffy. Gradually beat in **EAGLE BRAND®** until smooth. Add eggs and lemon juice; mix well. Pour into prepared crust.

**3.** Bake 50 to 55 minutes or until set. Remove from oven; top with sour cream. Bake 5 minutes longer. Cool. Chill. Prepare Raspberry Topping (optional) and serve with cheesecake. Store leftovers covered in refrigerator.

**New York Style Cheesecake:** Increase cream cheese to 4 (8-ounce) packages and eggs to 4. Proceed as directed, adding 2 tablespoons all-purpose flour after eggs. Bake 1 hour 10 minutes or until center is set. Omit sour cream. Cool. Chill. Serve and store as directed.

## RASPBERRY TOPPING

2 cups water

½ cup confectioners' sugar

¼ cup red raspberry jam

1 tablespoon cornstarch

1 cup frozen red raspberries

In small saucepan over medium heat, combine water, confectioners' sugar, jam and cornstarch. Cook and stir until thickened and clear. Cool. Stir in raspberries.

*Makes about 1⅓ cups*

# FESTIVE CRANBERRY
# CREAM CHEESE SQUARES

2 cups all-purpose flour

1½ cups oats

¾ cup plus 1 tablespoon firmly packed brown sugar, divided

1 cup (2 sticks) butter or margarine, softened

1 (8-ounce) package cream cheese, softened

1 (14-ounce) can **EAGLE BRAND®** Sweetened Condensed Milk (NOT evaporated milk)

2 eggs

1 (27-ounce) jar **NONE SUCH®** Ready-to-Use Mincemeat (Regular or Brandy & Rum)

2 tablespoons cornstarch

1 (16-ounce) can whole-berry cranberry sauce

**1.** Preheat oven to 375°F. Grease 15×10-inch jelly-roll pan. In large bowl, beat flour, oats, ¾ cup brown sugar and butter until crumbly. Reserving 1½ cups crumb mixture, press remaining mixture on bottom of prepared pan. Bake 15 minutes or until lightly browned.

**2.** In medium bowl, beat cream cheese until fluffy. Gradually beat in **EAGLE BRAND®** until smooth; beat in eggs. Spread over baked crust; top with **NONE SUCH®**.

**3.** Combine remaining 1 tablespoon brown sugar and cornstarch; stir in cranberry sauce. Spoon over mincemeat. Top with reserved crumb mixture. Bake 40 minutes or until golden. Cool. Chill. Cut into squares. Store leftovers covered in refrigerator.

# Apple Cinnamon Cheesecake

½ cup (1 stick) plus 1 tablespoon butter or margarine, softened, divided

¼ cup firmly packed light brown sugar

1 cup all-purpose flour

¼ cup quick-cooking oats

¼ cup finely chopped walnuts

½ teaspoon ground cinnamon

2 (8-ounce) packages cream cheese, softened

1 (14-ounce) can **EAGLE BRAND®** Sweetened Condensed Milk (NOT evaporated milk)

3 eggs

½ cup frozen apple juice concentrate, thawed

2 medium apples, cored and sliced

Cinnamon Apple Glaze (recipe follows)

**1.** Preheat oven to 300°F. In small bowl, beat ½ cup butter and brown sugar until fluffy. Add flour, oats, walnuts and cinnamon; mix well. Press firmly on bottom and halfway up side of 9-inch springform pan. Bake 10 minutes.

**2.** In large bowl, beat cream cheese until fluffy. Gradually beat in **EAGLE BRAND®** until smooth. Add eggs and apple juice concentrate; mix well. Pour into baked crust.

**3.** Bake 45 minutes or until center springs back when lightly touched. Cool.

**4.** In large skillet, cook apples in remaining 1 tablespoon butter until tender-crisp. Arrange on top of cheesecake; drizzle with Cinnamon Apple Glaze. Chill. Store leftovers covered in refrigerator.

## Cinnamon Apple Glaze

¼ cup frozen apple juice concentrate, thawed

1 teaspoon cornstarch

¼ teaspoon ground cinnamon

In small saucepan, combine ingredients; mix well. Over low heat, cook and stir until thickened.

*Makes about ¼ cup*

# Frozen Peppermint Cheesecake

2 cups finely crushed chocolate wafer cookies* or crème-filled chocolate sandwich cookies (about 24 cookies)

¼ cup granulated sugar

¼ cup (½ stick) butter or margarine, melted

1 (8-ounce) package cream cheese, softened

1 (14-ounce) can **EAGLE BRAND®** Sweetened Condensed Milk (NOT evaporated milk)

2 teaspoons peppermint extract

Red food coloring (optional)

2 cups whipping cream, whipped

Hot fudge ice cream topping** (optional)

*One 9-ounce package of chocolate wafer cookies yields 2 cups crumbs.*

**See recipe for Hot Fudge Sauce on page 129.*

**1.** Line 9-inch round cake pan or springform pan with foil, extending foil over edges of pan. In medium bowl, combine cookie crumbs and sugar. Add butter; mix well. Press crumb mixture firmly on bottom and halfway up side of prepared pan. Chill.

**2.** In large bowl, beat cream cheese until fluffy. Gradually beat in **EAGLE BRAND®** until smooth. Stir in peppermint extract and food coloring (optional); mix well. Fold in whipped cream. Pour into crust.

**3.** Cover; freeze 6 hours or until firm. When cheesecake is firm, use foil to lift out of pan; peel off foil. Garnish with topping (optional). Store leftovers covered in freezer.

# Harvest Apple Streusel Squares

2   cups graham cracker crumbs

¾   cup (1½ sticks) butter or margarine, melted

½   cup finely chopped pecans

1   (8-ounce) package cream cheese, softened

1   (14-ounce) can **EAGLE BRAND®** Sweetened Condensed Milk (NOT evaporated milk)

2   eggs

1   (21-ounce) can apple pie filling

½   cup firmly packed brown sugar

½   cup all-purpose flour

¼   teaspoon ground cinnamon

¼   cup (½ stick) cold butter or margarine

½   cup dried cranberries

⅓   cup chopped pecans

**1.** Preheat oven to 350°F. Line 13×9-inch baking pan with parchment paper. In small bowl, combine graham cracker crumbs, melted butter and finely chopped pecans. Press firmly on bottom of prepared pan.

**2.** In medium bowl, beat cream cheese until fluffy. Beat in **EAGLE BRAND®** and eggs. Pour over prepared crust. Spoon apple pie filling over cream cheese layer.

**3.** In medium bowl, combine brown sugar, flour and cinnamon. Cut in cold butter until mixture resembles coarse crumbs. Stir in cranberries and chopped pecans. Sprinkle over apple layer. Bake 35 to 40 minutes or until golden (do not overbake). Cool. Cut into squares. Store leftovers covered in refrigerator.

# Maple Pumpkin Cheesecake

*Makes one (9-inch) cheesecake*

1¼ cups graham cracker crumbs

¼ cup granulated sugar

¼ cup (½ stick) butter or margarine, melted

3 (8-ounce) packages cream cheese, softened

1 (14-ounce) can **EAGLE BRAND®** Sweetened Condensed Milk (NOT evaporated milk)

1 (15-ounce) can pumpkin (2 cups)

3 eggs

¼ cup pure maple syrup

1½ teaspoons ground cinnamon

1 teaspoon ground nutmeg

½ teaspoon salt

Maple Pecan Glaze (recipe follows)

**1.** Preheat oven to 325°F. Combine graham cracker crumbs, sugar and butter; press firmly on bottom of ungreased 9-inch springform pan.

**2.** In large bowl, beat cream cheese until fluffy. Gradually beat in **EAGLE BRAND®** until smooth. Add pumpkin, eggs, maple syrup, cinnamon, nutmeg and salt; mix well. Pour into crust.

**3.** Bake 1 hour 15 minutes or until center appears nearly set when shaken. Cool 1 hour. Cover and chill at least 4 hours. Top with chilled Maple Pecan Glaze. Store leftovers covered in refrigerator.

## Maple Pecan Glaze

1 cup (½ pint) whipping cream

¾ cup pure maple syrup

½ cup chopped pecans

In medium saucepan over medium-high heat, combine whipping cream and maple syrup; bring to a boil. Boil rapidly 15 to 20 minutes or until thickened, stirring occasionally. Add nuts. Cover and chill. Stir before using.

# Two-Tone Cheesecake Bars

2 cups finely crushed crème-filled chocolate sandwich cookies (about 24 cookies)

3 tablespoons butter or margarine, melted

3 (8-ounce) packages cream cheese, softened

1 (14-ounce) can **EAGLE BRAND®** Sweetened Condensed Milk (NOT evaporated milk)

3 eggs

2 teaspoons vanilla extract

2 (1-ounce) squares unsweetened chocolate, melted

Chocolate Glaze (recipe follows)

**1.** Preheat oven to 300°F. In medium bowl, combine cookie crumbs and butter; press firmly on bottom of ungreased 13×9-inch baking pan.

**2.** In large bowl, beat cream cheese until fluffy. Gradually beat in **EAGLE BRAND®** until smooth. Add eggs and vanilla; mix well. Pour half of batter evenly over prepared crust. Stir melted chocolate into remaining batter; spoon evenly over plain batter.

**3.** Bake 55 to 60 minutes or until set. Cool. Top with Chocolate Glaze. Chill. Cut into bars. Store leftovers covered in refrigerator.

## Chocolate Glaze

2 (1-ounce) squares unsweetened chocolate

2 tablespoons butter or margarine

⅛ teaspoon salt

1¾ cups sifted confectioners' sugar

3 tablespoons hot water or cream

In small heavy saucepan over low heat, combine chocolate, butter and salt; cook and stir until melted. Remove from heat, add sugar and hot water; mix well. Immediately spread over cheesecake.

*Makes about 1 cup*

# CELEBRATION LIME CHEESECAKE BARS

1¼ cups all-purpose flour

⅓ cup granulated sugar

7 tablespoons butter or margarine, softened and cut into ½-inch pieces

1 egg yolk, beaten

⅓ cup firmly packed flaked coconut

2 (8-ounce) packages cream cheese, softened

1 (14-ounce) can **EAGLE BRAND®** Sweetened Condensed Milk (NOT evaporated milk)

2 eggs

½ cup lime juice

Optional Toppings (recipes follow)

**1.** Preheat oven to 400°F. Grease 13×9-inch glass baking dish. With mixer, combine flour and sugar. Add butter and egg yolk; blend until combined. Mix in coconut. Press dough onto bottom of prepared dish. Bake 12 to 14 minutes or until edge of crust is golden brown. Reduce oven temperature to 350°F.

**2.** With mixer, beat cream cheese until fluffy. Gradually beat in **EAGLE BRAND®** until smooth. Add eggs; mix until just combined. Stir in lime juice. Pour batter over baked crust.

**3.** With oven at 350°F, bake 17 to 22 minutes or until center is set. Cool. Cover and chill 2 hours. Serve with topping (optional). Store leftovers covered in refrigerator.

## WHITE CHOCOLATE GLAZE WITH TOASTED COCONUT AND PECANS

¼ cup (½ stick) butter or margarine, divided

½ cup flaked coconut

⅓ cup chopped pecans

1¼ cups white chocolate chips or vanilla chips

¼ cup lime juice

**1.** In skillet, melt 1 tablespoon butter. Add coconut and pecans; cook and stir until coconut is light brown. Remove from heat. Cool.

**2.** In large bowl, combine white chocolate chips, lime juice and remaining butter. Microwave on MEDIUM-HIGH (80% power) 30 to 40 seconds. Mix until smooth.

**3.** Pour glaze over bars, spreading evenly. Top with coconut mixture.

## Mixed Fruit Salsa

- 1 mango, peeled, pitted and diced
- 1 cup chopped pineapple
- 1 cup diced strawberries
- 2 tablespoons lemon juice
- ¼ cup granulated sugar

Mix all ingredients in bowl. Chill at least one hour. Stir before serving.

*Makes 2½ cups*

## Quick Berry Sauce

- 1 cup raspberries
- 2 tablespoons lemon juice
- 2 tablespoons granulated sugar, or to taste
- 1 cup blueberries
- 1 cup diced strawberries

In large bowl, combine raspberries, lemon juice and sugar. Using large fork or potato masher, mash the berries to make a purée. Fold in blueberries and strawberries. Store covered in refrigerator.

*Makes 2½ cups*

## Quick Raspberry Sauce

- 2 (10- or 12-ounce) packages frozen raspberries, thawed
- ¼ cup granulated sugar
- 2 tablespoons lemon juice
- 2 tablespoons water

Combine all ingredients in food processor or blender and mix until smooth. Store covered in refrigerator.

*Makes 3 cups*

*Shown with White Chocolate Glaze with Toasted Coconut and Pecans*

# CHOCOLATE MINT CHEESECAKE BARS

2 cups finely crushed crème-filled chocolate sandwich cookies (about 24 cookies)

½ cup (1 stick) butter or margarine, melted

1 (8-ounce) package cream cheese, softened

1 (14-ounce) can **EAGLE BRAND®** Sweetened Condensed Milk (NOT evaporated milk)

2 eggs

1 tablespoon peppermint extract

½ cup semisweet chocolate chips

2 teaspoons shortening

14 thin crème de menthe candies, chopped

**1.** Preheat oven to 325°F. In medium bowl, combine cookie crumbs and butter; blend well. Press crumb mixture firmly on bottom of ungreased 9-inch square baking pan. Bake 6 minutes. Cool.

**2.** In medium bowl, beat cream cheese until fluffy. Gradually beat in **EAGLE BRAND®**, eggs and peppermint extract until smooth. Spread over cooled cookie base. Bake 25 to 30 minutes. Cool 20 minutes; chill.

**3.** In heavy saucepan over low heat, melt chocolate chips and shortening. Drizzle over chilled cheesecake bars. Sprinkle with chopped crème de menthe candies. Cut into bars. Store leftovers covered in refrigerator.

# Lemony Cheesecake Bars

*Makes 2 dozen bars*

- 1½ cups graham cracker crumbs
- ⅓ cup granulated sugar
- ⅓ cup finely chopped pecans
- ⅓ cup (⅔ stick) butter or margarine, melted
- 2 (8-ounce) packages cream cheese, softened

- 1 (14-ounce) can **EAGLE BRAND®** Sweetened Condensed Milk (NOT evaporated milk)
- 2 eggs
- ½ cup lemon juice

**1.** Preheat oven to 325°F. In medium bowl, combine graham cracker crumbs, sugar, pecans and butter. Reserve ⅓ cup crumb mixture. Press remaining crumb mixture firmly on bottom of ungreased 13×9-inch baking pan. Bake 6 minutes. Cool on wire rack.

**2.** In large bowl, beat cream cheese until fluffy. Gradually beat in **EAGLE BRAND®** until smooth. Add eggs; beat until just blended. Stir in lemon juice. Carefully spoon mixture on top of crust. Spoon reserved crumb mixture to make diagonal stripes on top of cheese mixture or sprinkle to cover.

**3.** Bake 30 minutes or until knife inserted near center comes out clean. Cool on wire rack 1 hour. Chill. Cut into bars. Store leftovers covered in refrigerator.

# Luscious Baked Chocolate Cheesecake

1¼ cups graham cracker crumbs

⅓ cup (⅔ stick) butter or margarine, melted

¼ cup granulated sugar

3 (8-ounce) packages cream cheese, softened

1 (14-ounce) can **EAGLE BRAND®** Sweetened Condensed Milk (NOT evaporated milk)

2 cups (12 ounces) semisweet chocolate chips or 8 (1-ounce) squares semisweet chocolate, melted

4 eggs

2 teaspoons vanilla extract

**1.** Preheat oven to 300°F. Combine graham cracker crumbs, butter and sugar; press firmly on bottom of ungreased 9-inch springform pan.

**2.** In large bowl, beat cream cheese until fluffy. Gradually beat in **EAGLE BRAND®** until smooth. Add melted chocolate, eggs and vanilla; mix well. Pour into crust.

**3.** Bake 65 minutes or until center is set. Cool to room temperature. Chill. Garnish as desired. Store leftovers covered in refrigerator.

# Strawberry Swirl Cheesecake Bars

*Makes 2 to 3 dozen bars*

1 (10-ounce) package
  frozen strawberries,
  thawed (2½ cups)

1 tablespoon cornstarch

1¾ cups cinnamon graham
  cracker crumbs

¼ cup (½ stick) butter or
  margarine, melted

2 (8-ounce) packages cream
  cheese, softened

1 (14-ounce) can **EAGLE BRAND**®
  Sweetened Condensed Milk
  (NOT evaporated milk)

2 eggs

⅓ cup lemon juice

1 teaspoon vanilla extract

**1.** Preheat oven to 350°F. Grease 13×9-inch baking pan. In blender container, blend strawberries until smooth. In saucepan over medium heat, combine strawberry purée and cornstarch; cook and stir until thickened. Cool.

**2.** In small bowl, combine graham cracker crumbs and butter; press firmly on bottom of prepared pan.

**3.** In large bowl, beat cream cheese until fluffy. Gradually beat in **EAGLE BRAND**® until smooth. Add eggs, lemon juice and vanilla; mix well. Pour over crust.

**4.** Drop strawberry mixture by spoonfuls over batter. Gently swirl with knife or spatula. Bake 25 to 30 minutes or until center is set. Cool. Chill. Cut into bars. Store leftovers covered in refrigerator.

# Toffee-Top Cheesecake Bars

*Makes about 3 dozen bars*

1¼ cups all-purpose flour

1 cup confectioners' sugar

½ cup unsweetened cocoa powder

¼ teaspoon baking soda

¾ cup (1½ sticks) butter or margarine, softened

1 (8-ounce) package cream cheese, softened

1 (14-ounce) can **EAGLE BRAND®** Sweetened Condensed Milk (NOT evaporated milk)

2 eggs

1 teaspoon vanilla extract

1¾ cups (10 ounces) English toffee bits, divided

**1.** Preheat oven to 350°F. In medium bowl, combine flour, confectioners' sugar, cocoa and baking soda; cut in butter until mixture is crumbly. Press firmly onto bottom of ungreased 13×9-inch baking pan. Bake 15 minutes.

**2.** In large bowl, beat cream cheese until fluffy. Add **EAGLE BRAND®**, eggs and vanilla; beat until smooth. Stir in 1 cup toffee bits. Pour mixture over hot crust. Bake 25 minutes or until set and edges just begin to brown.

**3.** Remove from oven. Cool 15 minutes. Sprinkle remaining ¾ cup toffee bits evenly over top. Cool completely. Refrigerate several hours or until cold. Cut into bars. Store leftovers covered in refrigerator.

# BROWNIE CHOCOLATE CHIP CHEESECAKE

*Makes one (9-inch) cheesecake*

1   (19.5- or 22-ounce) package fudge brownie mix

3   (8-ounce) packages cream cheese, softened

1   (14-ounce) can **EAGLE BRAND®** Sweetened Condensed Milk (NOT evaporated milk)

3   eggs

2   teaspoons vanilla extract

½   cup miniature semisweet chocolate chips

**1.** Preheat oven to 350°F. Grease bottom only of 9-inch springform pan. Prepare brownie mix as package directs for chewy brownies. Spread evenly in prepared pan. Bake 35 minutes or until set.

**2.** In large bowl, beat cream cheese until fluffy. Gradually beat in **EAGLE BRAND®** until smooth. Add eggs and vanilla; mix well. Stir in chocolate chips. Pour into baked crust.

**3.** Reduce oven temperature to 300°F. Bake 50 minutes or until set. Cool. Chill thoroughly. Remove side of springform pan. Garnish as desired. Store leftovers covered in refrigerator.

☐ **Note:** Chocolate chips may fall to top of brownie layer during baking.

# PUMPKIN CHEESECAKE BARS

- 1 (16-ounce) package pound cake mix
- 3 eggs, divided
- 2 tablespoons butter or margarine, melted
- 4 teaspoons pumpkin pie spice, divided
- 1 (8-ounce) package cream cheese, softened
- 1 (14-ounce) can **EAGLE BRAND®** Sweetened Condensed Milk (NOT evaporated milk)
- 1 (15-ounce) can pumpkin (2 cups)
- ½ teaspoon salt
- 1 cup chopped nuts

**1.** Preheat oven to 350°F. In large bowl with mixer on low speed, combine cake mix, 1 egg, butter and 2 teaspoons pumpkin pie spice until crumbly. Press onto bottom of ungreased 15×10-inch jelly-roll pan.

**2.** In large bowl, beat cream cheese until fluffy. Gradually beat in **EAGLE BRAND®** until smooth. Beat in remaining 2 eggs, pumpkin, remaining 2 teaspoons pumpkin pie spice and salt; mix well. Pour into prepared crust; sprinkle with nuts.

**3.** Bake 30 to 35 minutes or until set. Cool. Chill. Cut into bars. Store leftovers covered in refrigerator.

# COOKIES & BARS

## TOFFEE BARS

*Makes 2 to 3 dozen bars*

- 1 cup quick-cooking oats
- ½ cup all-purpose flour
- ½ cup firmly packed light brown sugar
- ½ cup finely chopped walnuts
- ½ cup (1 stick) butter or margarine, melted, divided
- ¼ teaspoon baking soda

- 1 (14-ounce) can **EAGLE BRAND®** Sweetened Condensed Milk (NOT evaporated milk)
- 2 teaspoons vanilla extract
- 2 cups (12 ounces) semisweet chocolate chips

  Additional chopped walnuts (optional)

**1.** Preheat oven to 350°F. Grease 13×9-inch baking pan. In large bowl, combine oats, flour, brown sugar, walnuts, 6 tablespoons butter and baking soda. Press firmly on bottom of prepared pan. Bake 10 to 15 minutes or until lightly browned.

**2.** In medium saucepan over medium heat, combine remaining 2 tablespoons butter and **EAGLE BRAND®**. Cook and stir until mixture thickens slightly, about 15 minutes. Remove from heat; stir in vanilla. Spread evenly over baked crust. Bake 10 to 15 minutes or until golden brown.

**3.** Remove from oven; immediately sprinkle with chocolate chips. Let stand 1 minute; spread chocolate chips while still warm. Garnish with additional walnuts (optional); press down firmly. Cool thoroughly. Chill if desired. Cut into bars. Store tightly covered at room temperature.

# CUT-OUT COOKIES

*Makes 5½ dozen cookies*

3½ cups all-purpose flour

2 teaspoons baking powder

¼ teaspoon salt

1 (14-ounce) can **EAGLE BRAND®** Sweetened Condensed Milk (NOT evaporated milk)

¾ cup (1½ sticks) butter or margarine, softened

2 eggs

1 tablespoon vanilla extract

Colored sugar sprinkles (optional)

Confectioners' Sugar Glaze (optional, recipe follows)

**1.** In small bowl, combine flour, baking powder and salt; set aside.

**2.** In large bowl with mixer on low speed, beat **EAGLE BRAND®**, butter, eggs and vanilla until just combined. Beat on medium speed 1 minute until smooth. Add flour mixture; beat on low speed until combined. (If using hand-held mixer, use wooden spoon to add last portion of flour mixture.)

**3.** Divide dough into thirds. Wrap and chill dough 2 hours or until easy to handle.

**4.** Preheat oven to 350°F. On lightly floured surface, roll out one portion of dough to ⅛-inch thickness. Cut out shapes with floured cookie cutters. Reroll as necessary to use all dough. Place cut-outs 1 inch apart on ungreased baking sheets. Sprinkle with colored sugar (optional).

**5.** Bake 9 to 11 minutes or until very lightly browned around edges (do not overbake). Cool 5 minutes; transfer cookies to wire racks. Glaze with Confectioners' Sugar Glaze (optional) and decorate as desired. Store leftovers loosely covered at room temperature, or freeze in tightly sealed container.

## CONFECTIONERS' SUGAR GLAZE

2 cups sifted confectioners' sugar

½ teaspoon vanilla extract

2 tablespoons milk or heavy cream

Food coloring (optional)

Whisk confectioners' sugar and vanilla, adding just enough milk to create desired glaze consistency. Add food coloring (optional) to tint glaze.

# WALNUT CARAMEL TRIANGLES

2 cups all-purpose flour

½ cup confectioners' sugar

1 cup (2 sticks) cold butter
  or margarine

1 (14-ounce) can **EAGLE BRAND®**
  Sweetened Condensed Milk
  (NOT evaporated milk)

½ cup whipping cream

1 teaspoon vanilla extract

1½ cups chopped walnuts

  Chocolate Drizzle
    (recipe follows)

**1.** Preheat oven to 350°F. In medium bowl, combine flour and confectioners' sugar; cut in butter until crumbly. Press firmly on bottom of ungreased 13×9-inch baking pan. Bake 15 minutes or until lightly browned around edges.

**2.** In heavy saucepan over medium-high heat, combine **EAGLE BRAND®**, whipping cream and vanilla. Cook and stir until mixture comes to a boil. Reduce heat to medium; cook and stir until mixture thickens, 8 to 10 minutes. Stir in walnuts. Spread evenly over prepared crust.

**3.** Bake 20 minutes or until golden brown. Cool. Garnish with Chocolate Drizzle. Chill. Cut into triangles. Store leftovers covered at room temperature.

## CHOCOLATE DRIZZLE

½ cup semisweet chocolate chips

1 teaspoon shortening

Melt chocolate chips with shortening. Carefully drizzle on with spoon.

# CANDY BAR BARS

¾ cup (1½ sticks) butter or margarine, softened

¼ cup peanut butter

1 cup firmly packed light brown sugar

1 teaspoon baking soda

2 cups quick-cooking oats

1½ cups all-purpose flour

1 egg

1 (14-ounce) can **EAGLE BRAND®** Sweetened Condensed Milk (NOT evaporated milk)

4 cups chopped candy bars (chocolate-covered caramel-topped nougat bars with peanuts, chocolate-covered crisp wafers, chocolate-covered caramel-topped cookie bars or chocolate-covered peanut butter cups)

**1.** Preheat oven to 350°F. In large bowl, combine butter and peanut butter until smooth. Add brown sugar and baking soda; beat well. Stir in oats and flour. Reserve 1¾ cups crumb mixture.

**2.** Stir egg into remaining crumb mixture in bowl. Press firmly on bottom of ungreased 15×10-inch baking pan. Bake 15 minutes. Remove from oven.

**3.** Spread **EAGLE BRAND®** over hot crust. Stir together reserved crumb mixture and candy bar pieces; sprinkle evenly over top.

**4.** Bake 25 minutes or until golden brown. Cool. Cut into bars. Store leftovers loosely covered at room temperature.

# Double Chocolate Cherry Cookies

*Makes about 6 dozen cookies*

3½  cups all-purpose flour

¾  cup unsweetened cocoa powder

½  teaspoon baking powder

½  teaspoon baking soda

¼  teaspoon salt

1¼  cups (2½ sticks) butter or margarine, softened

1¾  cups granulated sugar

2  eggs

1  tablespoon vanilla extract

2  (6-ounce) jars maraschino cherries (without stems), well drained and halved (about 72 cherry halves)

1  cup (6 ounces) semisweet chocolate chips

1  (14-ounce) can **EAGLE BRAND®** Sweetened Condensed Milk (NOT evaporated milk)

**1.** Preheat oven to 350°F. In large bowl, combine flour, cocoa, baking powder, baking soda and salt; set aside.

**2.** In large bowl, beat butter and sugar until fluffy. Add eggs and vanilla; mix well. Stir in flour mixture (dough will be stiff). Shape into 1-inch balls. Place 1 inch apart on ungreased baking sheets. Press cherry half into center of each cookie. Bake 8 to 10 minutes. Cool.

**3.** In heavy saucepan over low heat, melt chocolate chips with **EAGLE BRAND®**; continue cooking about 3 minutes or until mixture thickens.

**4.** Frost each cookie, covering cherry. Store leftovers loosely covered at room temperature.

**Double Chocolate Pecan Cookies:** Prepare cookies as directed, omitting cherries; flatten. Bake as directed and frost tops. Garnish each cookie with pecan half.

# PETITE MACAROON CUPS

*Makes 4 dozen cups*

1 cup (2 sticks) butter or margarine, softened

2 (3-ounce) packages cream cheese, softened

2 cups all-purpose flour

1 (14-ounce) can **EAGLE BRAND®** Sweetened Condensed Milk (NOT evaporated milk)

2 eggs, beaten

1½ teaspoons vanilla extract

½ teaspoon almond extract

1⅓ cups flaked coconut

**1.** In large bowl, beat butter and cream cheese until fluffy; stir in flour. Cover; chill 1 hour.

**2.** Preheat oven to 375°F. Divide dough into quarters. On floured surface, shape 1 quarter into smooth ball. Divide into 12 balls. Place each ball in ungreased 1¾-inch mini muffin cup; press evenly on bottom and up side of each cup. Repeat with remaining dough.

**3.** In medium bowl, combine **EAGLE BRAND®**, eggs, vanilla and almond extracts; mix well. Stir in coconut. Fill muffin cups three-fourths full. Bake 16 to 18 minutes or until slightly browned. Cool in pans. Remove from pan using small metal spatula or knife. Store leftovers loosely covered at room temperature.

**Chocolate Macaroon Cups:** Beat ¼ cup unsweetened cocoa powder into egg mixture; proceed as above.

# CHOCOLATE 'N OAT BARS

1 cup all-purpose flour

1 cup quick-cooking oats

¾ cup firmly packed light brown sugar

½ cup (1 stick) butter or margarine, softened

1 (14-ounce) can **EAGLE BRAND®** Sweetened Condensed Milk (NOT evaporated milk)

1 cup chopped nuts

1 cup (6 ounces) semisweet chocolate chips

**1.** Preheat oven to 350°F (325°F for glass dish). In large bowl, combine flour, oats, brown sugar and butter; mix well. (Mixture will be crumbly.) Reserve ½ cup oat mixture. Press remaining mixture firmly on bottom of ungreased 13×9-inch baking pan. Bake 10 minutes. Remove from oven.

**2.** Pour **EAGLE BRAND®** evenly over crust. Sprinkle with nuts and chocolate chips. Top with reserved oat mixture; press down firmly.

**3.** Bake 25 minutes or until lightly browned. Cool. Chill if desired. Cut into bars. Store leftovers covered at room temperature.

# Seven-Layer Magic Cookie Bars

*Makes 2 to 3 dozen bars*

1½ cups graham cracker crumbs

½ cup (1 stick) butter or margarine, melted

1 (14-ounce) can **EAGLE BRAND®** Sweetened Condensed Milk (NOT evaporated milk)

1 cup (6 ounces) semisweet chocolate chips

1 cup (6 ounces) butterscotch chips

1⅓ cups flaked coconut

1 cup chopped nuts

**1.** Preheat oven to 350°F (325°F for glass baking pan). In small bowl, combine graham cracker crumbs and butter; mix well. Press firmly on bottom of ungreased 13×9-inch baking pan.

**2.** Pour **EAGLE BRAND®** evenly over crumb mixture. Layer evenly with remaining ingredients; press down firmly with fork.

**3.** Bake 25 minutes or until lightly browned. Cool. Chill if desired. Cut into bars or diamonds. Store leftovers covered at room temperature.

**TIP:** Peanut butter chips or white chocolate chips can be substituted for butterscotch chips.

# ALMOND FUDGE-TOPPED SHORTBREAD

*Makes 2 to 3 dozen bars*

1 cup (2 sticks) butter or margarine, softened

½ cup confectioners' sugar

¼ teaspoon salt

1¼ cups all-purpose flour

2 cups (12 ounces) semisweet chocolate chips

1 (14-ounce) can **EAGLE BRAND®** Sweetened Condensed Milk (NOT evaporated milk)

½ teaspoon almond extract

Sliced almonds, toasted

**1.** Preheat oven to 350°F. Grease 13×9-inch baking pan. In large bowl, beat butter, confectioners' sugar and salt until fluffy. Add flour; mix well.

**2.** With floured hands, press evenly into prepared pan. Bake 20 to 25 minutes or until lightly browned.

**3.** In heavy saucepan over low heat, melt chocolate chips with **EAGLE BRAND®**, stirring constantly. Remove from heat; stir in almond extract. Spread evenly over shortbread.

**4.** Garnish with almonds; press down firmly. Chill 3 hours or until firm. Cut into bars. Store leftovers covered at room temperature.

**TIP:** To toast almonds, spread in single layer in heavy-bottomed skillet. Cook over medium heat 1 to 2 minutes, stirring frequently, until nuts are lightly browned. Remove from skillet immediately. Cool before using.

# PEANUT BUTTER BLOSSOM COOKIES

*Makes about 5½ dozen cookies*

1  (14-ounce) can **EAGLE BRAND®** Sweetened Condensed Milk (NOT evaporated milk)

¾  cup peanut butter

2  cups biscuit baking mix

1  teaspoon vanilla extract

⅓  cup granulated sugar

65  solid milk chocolate candy pieces, unwrapped

**1.** Preheat oven to 375°F. In large bowl, beat **EAGLE BRAND®** and peanut butter until smooth. Add biscuit mix and vanilla; mix well.

**2.** Shape into 1-inch balls. Roll in sugar. Place 2 inches apart on ungreased baking sheets.

**3.** Bake 6 to 8 minutes or until lightly browned around edges (do not overbake). Immediately press chocolate candy piece into center of each cookie. Cool. Store leftovers tightly covered at room temperature.

# CHOCOLATE PEANUT BUTTER CHIP COOKIES

*Makes about 4 dozen cookies*

8 (1-ounce) squares semisweet chocolate

3 tablespoons butter or margarine

1 (14-ounce) can **EAGLE BRAND**® Sweetened Condensed Milk (NOT evaporated milk)

2 cups biscuit baking mix

1 egg

1 teaspoon vanilla extract

1 cup (6 ounces) peanut butter chips

**1.** Preheat oven to 350°F. In large saucepan over low heat, melt chocolate and butter with **EAGLE BRAND**®. Remove from heat.

**2.** Add biscuit mix, egg and vanilla; with mixer, beat until smooth and well blended. Let mixture cool to room temperature. Stir in peanut butter chips.

**3.** Drop by rounded teaspoonfuls onto ungreased baking sheets. Bake 6 to 8 minutes or until tops are lightly crusted. Cool. Store leftovers tightly covered at room temperature.

# Coconut Macaroons

**Makes about 4 dozen cookies**

1 (14-ounce) can **EAGLE BRAND**®
   Sweetened Condensed Milk
   (NOT evaporated milk)

1 egg white, whipped

2 teaspoons vanilla extract

1½ teaspoons almond extract

1 (14-ounce) package
   flaked coconut

**1.** Preheat oven to 325°F. Line baking sheets with foil; grease and flour foil; set aside.

**2.** In large bowl, combine **EAGLE BRAND**®, egg white, vanilla and almond extracts and coconut; mix well. Drop by rounded teaspoonfuls onto prepared baking sheets; slightly flatten each mound with a spoon.

**3.** Bake 15 to 17 minutes or until lightly browned around edges. Immediately remove from baking sheets (macaroons will stick if allowed to cool on baking sheets); cool on wire racks. Store loosely covered at room temperature.

# Golden Peanut Butter Bars

*Makes 2 to 3 dozen bars*

2 cups all-purpose flour

¾ cup firmly packed light brown sugar

1 egg, beaten

½ cup (1 stick) cold butter or margarine

1 cup chopped peanuts

1 (14-ounce) can **EAGLE BRAND®** Sweetened Condensed Milk (NOT evaporated milk)

½ cup peanut butter

1 teaspoon vanilla extract

**1.** Preheat oven to 350°F. In large bowl, combine flour, brown sugar and egg; cut in butter until crumbly. Stir in peanuts. Reserve 2 cups crumb mixture. Press remaining mixture on bottom of ungreased 13×9-inch baking pan. Bake 15 minutes or until lightly browned.

**2.** In large bowl, with mixer, beat **EAGLE BRAND®**, peanut butter and vanilla. Spread over prepared crust; top with reserved crumb mixture.

**3.** Bake 25 minutes or until lightly browned. Cool. Chill if desired. Cut into bars. Store leftovers covered at room temperature.

# HOLIDAY TREASURE COOKIES

*Makes about 5½ dozen cookies*

1½ cups graham cracker crumbs

½ cup all-purpose flour

2 teaspoons baking powder

1 (14-ounce) can **EAGLE BRAND®** Sweetened Condensed Milk (NOT evaporated milk)

½ cup (1 stick) butter or margarine, softened

1⅓ cups flaked coconut

1¾ cups (10 ounces) mini kisses, milk chocolate or semisweet chocolate baking pieces

1 cup red and green holiday baking bits

**1.** Preheat oven to 375°F. Grease cookie sheets. In medium bowl, combine graham cracker crumbs, flour and baking powder; set aside.

**2.** Beat **EAGLE BRAND®** and butter until smooth; add reserved crumb mixture, mixing well. Stir in coconut, chocolate pieces and holiday baking bits. Drop by rounded teaspoonfuls onto prepared cookie sheets.

**3.** Bake 7 to 9 minutes or until lightly browned. Cool 1 minute; transfer from cookie sheet to wire rack. Cool completely. Store leftovers tightly covered at room temperature.

# LEMON CRUMB BARS

*Makes 2 to 3 dozen bars*

1 (18.25- or 18.5-ounce) package lemon or yellow cake mix

½ cup (1 stick) butter or margarine, softened

1 egg

2 cups finely crushed saltine crackers

1 (14-ounce) can **EAGLE BRAND®** Sweetened Condensed Milk (NOT evaporated milk)

½ cup lemon juice

3 egg yolks

**1.** Preheat oven to 350°F. Grease 13×9-inch baking pan. In large bowl, combine cake mix, butter and 1 egg with mixer until crumbly. Stir in cracker crumbs. Reserve 2 cups crumb mixture. Press remaining crumb mixture firmly on bottom of prepared pan. Bake 15 to 20 minutes or until golden.

**2.** With mixer or wire whisk, beat **EAGLE BRAND®**, lemon juice and 3 egg yolks. Spread evenly over prepared crust. Top with reserved crumb mixture.

**3.** Bake 20 minutes longer or until set and top is golden. Cool. Cut into bars. Store leftovers covered in refrigerator.

> **TIP:** You can easily make cracker crumbs by crumbling the crackers into a food processor fitted with a metal blade; process until fine crumbs form. If you prefer, you can put the crackers in a resealable plastic food storage bag, then use a rolling pin to crush them into crumbs.

# Magic Cookie Bars

*Makes 2 to 3 dozen bars*

1½ cups graham cracker crumbs

½ cup (1 stick) butter or margarine, melted

1 (14-ounce) can **EAGLE BRAND**® Sweetened Condensed Milk (NOT evaporated milk)

2 cups (12 ounces) semisweet chocolate chips

1⅓ cups flaked coconut

1 cup chopped nuts

**1.** Preheat oven to 350°F (325°F for glass baking dish). In small bowl, combine graham cracker crumbs and butter; mix well. Press crumb mixture firmly on bottom of ungreased 13×9-inch baking pan.

**2.** Pour **EAGLE BRAND**® evenly over crumb mixture. Layer evenly with remaining ingredients; press down firmly with fork.

**3.** Bake 25 minutes or until lightly browned. Cool. Chill if desired. Cut into bars or diamonds. Store covered at room temperature.

**Magic Rainbow Cookie Bars:** Substitute 2 cups plain candy-coated chocolate pieces for semisweet chocolate chips.

**Magic Peanut Cookie Bars:** Substitute 2 cups (about ¾ pound) chocolate-covered peanuts for semisweet chocolate chips and chopped nuts.

# PECAN PIE BARS

2 cups all-purpose flour

¼ cup firmly packed brown sugar

½ cup (1 stick) cold butter

1½ cups chopped pecans

1 (14-ounce) can **EAGLE BRAND®** Sweetened Condensed Milk (NOT evaporated milk)

3 eggs, beaten

2 tablespoons lemon juice

**1.** Preheat oven to 350°F. In medium bowl, combine flour and brown sugar; cut in butter until crumbly. Press firmly on bottom of ungreased 13×9-inch baking pan. Bake 10 to 15 minutes.

**2.** In large bowl, combine pecans, **EAGLE BRAND®**, eggs and lemon juice; pour over crust.

**3.** Bake 25 minutes or until filling is set. Cool. Chill if desired. Cut into bars. Store covered at room temperature.

# CHOCOLATE MAPLE NUT BARS

*Makes 2 to 3 dozen bars*

1½ cups all-purpose flour

⅔ cup granulated sugar

½ teaspoon salt

¾ cup (1½ sticks) cold butter or margarine

2 eggs, divided

1 (14-ounce) can **EAGLE BRAND®** Sweetened Condensed Milk (NOT evaporated milk)

1½ teaspoons maple flavoring

2 cups chopped nuts

1 cup (6 ounces) semisweet chocolate chips

**1.** Preheat oven to 350°F. In large bowl, combine flour, sugar and salt; cut in butter until crumbly. Stir in 1 beaten egg. Press firmly on bottom of ungreased 13×9-inch baking pan. Bake 25 minutes.

**2.** In medium bowl, beat **EAGLE BRAND®**, remaining egg and maple flavoring; stir in nuts.

**3.** Sprinkle chocolate chips evenly over prepared crust. Top with nut mixture; bake 25 minutes or until golden. Cool. Cut into bars. Store leftovers tightly covered at room temperature.

# CHOCOLATE CHIP TREASURE COOKIES

*Makes about 3 dozen cookies*

| | | | |
|---|---|---|---|
| 1½ | cups graham cracker crumbs | ½ | cup (1 stick) butter or margarine, softened |
| ½ | cup all-purpose flour | 2 | cups (12 ounces) semisweet chocolate chips |
| 2 | teaspoons baking powder | | |
| 1 | (14-ounce) can **EAGLE BRAND®** Sweetened Condensed Milk (NOT evaporated milk) | 1⅓ | cups flaked coconut |
| | | 1 | cup chopped walnuts |

**1.** Preheat oven to 375°F. In small bowl, combine graham cracker crumbs, flour and baking powder; set aside.

**2.** In large bowl, beat **EAGLE BRAND®** and butter until smooth. Add crumb mixture; mix well. Stir in chocolate chips, coconut and walnuts.

**3.** Drop by rounded tablespoonfuls onto ungreased baking sheets. Bake 9 to 10 minutes or until lightly browned. Cool. Store loosely covered at room temperature.

# CHOCOLATE FANTASY BARS

*Makes 2 to 3 dozen bars*

1 (18.25- or 18.5-ounce) package chocolate cake mix

⅓ cup vegetable oil

1 egg

1 cup chopped nuts

1 cup (6 ounces) semisweet chocolate chips

1 (14-ounce) can **EAGLE BRAND®** Sweetened Condensed Milk (NOT evaporated milk)

1 teaspoon vanilla extract

⅛ teaspoon salt

1 tube decorating icing (optional)

**1.** Preheat oven to 350°F. Grease 13×9-inch baking pan. In large bowl, with mixer on medium speed, beat cake mix, oil and egg until crumbly. Stir in nuts. Reserve 1 cup crumb mixture. Press remaining mixture firmly on bottom of prepared pan.

**2.** In small saucepan over low heat, melt chocolate chips with **EAGLE BRAND®**, vanilla and salt. Pour evenly over prepared crust. Sprinkle reserved crumb mixture evenly over top.

**3.** Bake 25 to 30 minutes or until edges are firm. Cool. Cut into bars. Drizzle with icing (optional). Store loosely covered at room temperature.

# DESSERT FAVORITES

## CHOCOLATE MOUSSE & RASPBERRIES

4 (1-ounce) squares unsweetened chocolate

1 (14-ounce) can **EAGLE BRAND®** Sweetened Condensed Milk (NOT evaporated milk)

2 teaspoons vanilla extract

2 cups (1 pint) whipping cream, whipped

⅔ cup water

¼ cup red raspberry jam

3 tablespoons confectioners' sugar

1 tablespoon cornstarch

1 cup frozen raspberries

**1.** In large heavy saucepan over medium-low heat, melt chocolate with **EAGLE BRAND®**; stir in vanilla. Pour into large bowl; cool to room temperature, about 1½ hours.

**2.** Beat chocolate mixture until smooth. Fold in whipped cream. Spoon into 8 to 10 individual dessert dishes. Chill.

**3.** In small saucepan, combine water, jam, confectioners' sugar and cornstarch. Cook and stir until thickened and clear. Cool. Stir in raspberries.

**4.** Top each serving with raspberry topping and serve. Store leftovers covered in refrigerator.

# Dutch Apple Dessert

*Makes 6 to 8 servings*

5   medium apples, peeled, cored and sliced

1   (14-ounce) can **EAGLE BRAND®** Sweetened Condensed Milk (NOT evaporated milk)

1   teaspoon ground cinnamon

½   cup (1 stick) plus 2 tablespoons cold butter or margarine, divided

1½  cups biscuit baking mix, divided

½   cup firmly packed brown sugar

½   cup chopped nuts

  Ice cream (optional)

**1.** Preheat oven to 325°F. Grease 9-inch square baking pan. In medium bowl, combine apples, **EAGLE BRAND®** and cinnamon.

**2.** In large bowl, cut ½ cup butter into 1 cup biscuit mix until crumbly. Stir in apple mixture. Pour into prepared pan.

**3.** In small bowl, combine remaining ½ cup biscuit mix and brown sugar. Cut in 2 tablespoons butter until crumbly; add nuts. Sprinkle evenly over apple mixture.

**4.** Bake 1 hour or until golden. Serve warm with ice cream (optional). Store leftovers covered in refrigerator.

**Microwave Method:** In 2-quart round baking dish, prepare as directed above. Microwave on HIGH (100% power) 14 to 15 minutes, rotating dish after 7 minutes. Let stand 5 minutes.

# Holiday Pumpkin Treats

*Makes 1 to 2 dozen bars*

1¾ cups all-purpose flour

⅓ cup granulated sugar

⅓ cup firmly packed light brown sugar

1 cup (2 sticks) cold butter or margarine

1 cup finely chopped nuts

1 (27-ounce) jar **NONE SUCH®** Ready-to-Use Mincemeat (Regular or Brandy & Rum)

1 (15-ounce) can pumpkin (2 cups)

1 (14-ounce) can **EAGLE BRAND®** Sweetened Condensed Milk (NOT evaporated milk)

2 eggs

1 teaspoon ground cinnamon

½ teaspoon ground allspice

½ teaspoon salt

**1.** Preheat oven to 425°F. Combine flour and sugars; cut in butter until crumbly. Stir in nuts. Reserve 1½ cups crumb mixture. Press remaining crumb mixture on bottom and halfway up sides of ungreased 13×9-inch baking pan. Spoon **NONE SUCH®** over crust.

**2.** Combine pumpkin, **EAGLE BRAND®**, eggs, cinnamon, allspice and salt; mix until smooth. Pour over **NONE SUCH®**. Top with reserved crumb mixture.

**3.** Bake 15 minutes. Reduce oven temperature to 350°F. Bake 40 minutes longer or until golden brown around edges. Cool. Cut into squares. Serve warm or at room temperature. Store leftovers covered in refrigerator.

# STRAWBERRY SUNDAE DESSERT

2 cups finely crushed chocolate wafer cookies* or crème-filled chocolate sandwich cookies (about 24 cookies)

½ cup (1 stick) butter or margarine, melted

1 (14-ounce) can **EAGLE BRAND®** Sweetened Condensed Milk (NOT evaporated milk)

1 tablespoon vanilla extract

2 cups (1 pint) whipping cream, whipped

2 (10-ounce) packages frozen strawberries, thawed (5 cups)

¼ cup granulated sugar

1 tablespoon lemon juice

2 teaspoons cornstarch

*One 9-ounce package of chocolate wafer cookies yields 2 cups crumbs.

**1.** In small bowl, combine wafer crumbs and butter. Press half of crumb mixture on bottom of ungreased 9-inch square baking pan.

**2.** In large bowl, combine **EAGLE BRAND®** and vanilla. Fold in whipped cream. Pour into crust.

**3.** In blender or food processor, combine strawberries, sugar and lemon juice; blend until smooth. Spoon ¾ cup strawberry mixture evenly over cream mixture. Top with remaining crumb mixture. Cover; freeze 6 hours or until firm.

**4.** In small saucepan, over medium heat, combine remaining strawberry mixture and cornstarch. Cook and stir until thickened. Cool. Chill.

**5.** Cut dessert into squares; serve with sauce. Store leftovers covered in freezer; refrigerate any leftover sauce.

# CREAMY CINNAMON ROLLS

*Makes 12 rolls*

2 (1-pound) loaves frozen bread dough, thawed

⅔ cup (half of 14-ounce can*) **EAGLE BRAND®** Sweetened Condensed Milk (NOT evaporated milk), divided

1 cup chopped pecans

2 teaspoons ground cinnamon

1 cup confectioners' sugar

½ teaspoon vanilla extract

Additional chopped pecans (optional)

*Use remaining **EAGLE BRAND®** as a dip for fruit. Pour into storage container and store tightly covered in refrigerator for up to 1 week.*

**1.** On lightly floured surface, roll each bread dough loaf into 12×9-inch rectangle. Spread ⅓ cup **EAGLE BRAND®** over dough rectangles. Cover and chill remaining **EAGLE BRAND®**. Sprinkle rectangles with 1 cup pecans and cinnamon. Roll up jelly-roll-style, starting from short side. Cut each log into 6 slices.

**2.** Place rolls, cut sides down, in well-greased 13×9-inch baking pan. Cover loosely with greased wax paper and then with plastic wrap. Chill overnight.

**3.** Let pan of rolls stand at room temperature 30 minutes. Preheat oven to 350°F. Bake 30 to 35 minutes or until golden brown. Cool in pan 5 minutes; loosen edges and remove rolls from pan.

**4.** In small bowl, combine confectioners' sugar, remaining ⅓ cup **EAGLE BRAND®** and vanilla. Drizzle frosting over warm rolls. Sprinkle with additional chopped pecans (optional).

# Citrus-Filled Meringues

8  (3-inch) Meringue Shells (recipe follows)

1  (14-ounce) can **EAGLE BRAND®** Sweetened Condensed Milk (NOT evaporated milk)

½  cup frozen limeade concentrate, thawed

2  tablespoons lemon juice

2  egg yolks

Green or yellow food coloring (optional)

1  (4-ounce) container frozen nondairy whipped topping, thawed (about 1¾ cups)

**1.** Prepare Meringue Shells in advance.

**2.** In medium saucepan, combine **EAGLE BRAND®**, limeade, lemon juice and egg yolks; mix well. Over medium heat, cook and stir rapidly until hot and slightly thickened. Remove from heat; cool 15 minutes. Chill.

**3.** Stir in food coloring (optional). Fold in whipped topping. Chill until ready to serve. Spoon into Meringue Shells just before serving. Garnish as desired. Store leftovers covered in refrigerator.

## Meringue Shells

3  egg whites, at room temperature

1  teaspoon vanilla extract

¼  teaspoon cream of tartar

¼  teaspoon salt

¾  cup granulated sugar

**1.** Preheat oven to 250°F. Cover baking sheets with parchment paper. Draw 8 (3-inch) circles about 2 inches apart on paper; set aside.

**2.** In large bowl, combine egg whites, vanilla, cream of tartar and salt. Beat with electric mixer on medium speed until soft peaks form. On high speed, gradually beat in sugar until stiff but not dry. With pastry bag and star tip, pipe meringue within circles on paper; pipe rim to form shell. (Or spoon meringue within the circles, forming a hollow in center.)

**3.** Bake 1 hour. Turn off oven; leave meringues in oven 1 hour. Cool at room temperature. Store tightly covered at room temperature.

*Makes 8 shells*

# CLASSIC VANILLA ICE CREAM

*Makes about 1½ quarts*

1 vanilla bean or 2 tablespoons vanilla extract

2 cups (1 pint) half-and-half

2 cups (1 pint) whipping cream

1 (14-ounce) can **EAGLE BRAND®** Sweetened Condensed Milk (NOT evaporated milk)

**1.** Split vanilla bean lengthwise and scrape out seeds (or use vanilla extract). In large bowl, combine vanilla seeds or extract, half-and-half, whipping cream and **EAGLE BRAND®**; mix well.

**2.** Pour into ice cream freezer container. Freeze according to manufacturer's instructions. Store leftovers covered in freezer.

**Refrigerator-freezer method:** Omit half-and-half. Whip whipping cream. In large bowl, combine **EAGLE BRAND®** and vanilla. Fold in whipped cream. Pour into 9×5-inch loaf pan or other 2-quart container. Cover. Freeze 6 hours or until firm. Store leftovers covered in freezer.

**Fantastic Sundaes:** Top scoops of vanilla ice cream with flavored syrups, fresh fruits, crushed candies or crumbled cookies. Add a dollop of whipped cream and the ever-popular cherry. (See recipe for Hot Fudge Sauce on page 129; see recipe for Chocolate Peanut Butter Dessert Sauce on page 138.)

**Homemade Ice Cream Sandwiches:** Place a scoop of vanilla ice cream on a homemade or packaged cookie; top with another cookie. For a festive touch, roll the sandwich edge in crushed candy, chopped nuts or toasted coconut. Wrap individually in foil and freeze.

**À la Mode Desserts:** Design your own signature desserts by topping brownies, waffles or pound cake slices with a scoop of vanilla ice cream and fresh fruit, syrup or nuts.

**Delicious Homemade Milkshakes:** Combine 2 large scoops of vanilla ice cream with 1 cup milk in blender; blend in flavored syrups or fruits, if desired.

# DOUBLE CHOCOLATE ICE CREAM SQUARES

1½ cups finely crushed crème-filled chocolate sandwich cookies (about 18 cookies)

2 to 3 tablespoons butter or margarine, melted

1 (14-ounce) can **EAGLE BRAND®** Sweetened Condensed Milk (NOT evaporated milk)

3 (1-ounce) squares unsweetened chocolate, melted

2 teaspoons vanilla extract

1 cup chopped nuts (optional)

2 cups (1 pint) whipping cream, whipped

Whipped topping

Additional chopped nuts (optional)

**1.** In medium bowl, combine cookie crumbs and butter; press firmly on bottom of ungreased 13×9-inch baking pan.

**2.** In large bowl, beat **EAGLE BRAND®**, melted chocolate and vanilla until well blended. Stir in nuts (optional). Fold in whipped cream. Pour into crust. Spread with whipped topping.

**3.** Cover; freeze 6 hours or until firm. Garnish with additional chopped nuts (optional) or as desired. Store leftovers covered in freezer.

**Rocky Road Ice Cream Squares:** Add 1 cup miniature marshmallows to **EAGLE BRAND®** mixture. Proceed as directed above.

# Vanilla Mint Cream Puffs

12 Cream Puffs (recipe follows)

1 (14-ounce) can **EAGLE BRAND®** Sweetened Condensed Milk (NOT evaporated milk)

2 tablespoons white crème de menthe liqueur

2 tablespoons cold water

1 (4-serving size) package instant vanilla pudding and pie filling mix

1 cup (½ pint) whipping cream, whipped

Confectioners' sugar

Hot Fudge Sauce (optional, recipe follows)

**1.** Prepare Cream Puffs in advance.

**2.** In large bowl, combine **EAGLE BRAND®**, liqueur and water. Add pudding mix; beat well. Chill 5 minutes. Fold in whipped cream. Chill.

**3.** Just before serving, fill cream puffs; sprinkle with confectioners' sugar. Serve with Hot Fudge Sauce (optional). Store leftovers covered in refrigerator.

## Cream Puffs

1 cup water

½ cup (1 stick) butter or margarine

1 cup all-purpose flour

4 eggs

**1.** Preheat oven to 400°F. In medium saucepan, heat water and butter to a rolling boil. Stir in flour. Reduce heat to low; stir rapidly until mixture forms a ball, about 1 minute. Remove from heat. Add eggs; beat until smooth.

**2.** Using about ¼ cup for each puff, drop dough 3 inches apart onto ungreased baking sheets.

**3.** Bake 35 to 40 minutes or until puffed and golden. Cool. To serve, split and remove any dough from centers of puffs.

*Makes 12 puffs*

## Hot Fudge Sauce

- 1 cup (6 ounces) semisweet chocolate chips or 4 (1-ounce) squares semisweet chocolate
- 2 tablespoons butter or margarine
- 1 (14-ounce) can **EAGLE BRAND**® Sweetened Condensed Milk (NOT evaporated milk)
- 2 tablespoons water
- 1 teaspoon vanilla extract

In heavy saucepan over medium heat, melt chocolate chips and butter with **EAGLE BRAND**® and water. Cook and stir constantly until thickened, about 5 minutes. Add vanilla. Serve warm over cream puffs. Store leftovers covered in refrigerator.

*Makes about 2 cups*

# BLUEBERRY STREUSEL COBBLER

*Makes 8 to 12 servings*

- 1 pint fresh or frozen blueberries
- 1 (14-ounce) can **EAGLE BRAND®** Sweetened Condensed Milk (NOT evaporated milk)
- 2 teaspoons grated lemon rind
- ¾ cup (1½ sticks) plus 2 tablespoons cold butter or margarine, divided
- 2 cups biscuit baking mix, divided
- ½ cup firmly packed light brown sugar
- ½ cup chopped nuts
- Vanilla ice cream
- Blueberry Sauce (recipe follows)

**1.** Preheat oven to 325°F. Grease 9-inch square baking pan. In medium bowl, combine blueberries, **EAGLE BRAND®** and lemon rind.

**2.** In large bowl, cut ¾ cup butter into 1½ cups biscuit mix until crumbly; stir in blueberry mixture. Spread in prepared pan.

**3.** In small bowl, combine remaining ½ cup biscuit mix and brown sugar; cut in remaining 2 tablespoons butter until crumbly. Stir in nuts. Sprinkle over batter.

**4.** Bake 65 to 70 minutes. Serve warm with vanilla ice cream and Blueberry Sauce. Store leftovers covered in refrigerator.

## BLUEBERRY SAUCE

- ½ cup granulated sugar
- 1 tablespoon cornstarch
- ½ teaspoon ground cinnamon
- ¼ teaspoon ground nutmeg
- ½ cup water
- 1 pint fresh or frozen blueberries

In saucepan over medium heat, combine sugar, cornstarch, cinnamon and nutmeg. Gradually add water. Cook and stir until thickened. Stir in 1 pint blueberries; cook and stir until hot.

*Makes about 1⅔ cups*

# MINT CHOCOLATE CHIP ICE CREAM

*Makes about 1½ quarts*

1   (14-ounce) can **EAGLE BRAND®** Sweetened Condensed Milk (NOT evaporated milk)

2   teaspoons peppermint extract

Green food coloring (optional)

2   cups (1 pint) half-and-half

2   cups (1 pint) whipping cream

¾   cup miniature semisweet chocolate chips

**1.** In large bowl, combine **EAGLE BRAND®**, peppermint extract and food coloring (optional); mix well. Stir in remaining ingredients.

**2.** Pour into ice cream freezer container. Freeze according to manufacturer's instructions. Store leftovers covered in freezer.

**Refrigerator-freezer method:** Omit half-and-half. Whip whipping cream. In large bowl, combine **EAGLE BRAND®**, peppermint extract and food coloring (optional); mix well. Fold in whipped cream and ½ cup miniature chocolate chips. Pour into 9×5-inch loaf pan or other 2-quart container. Cover. Freeze 6 hours or until firm. Store leftovers covered in freezer.

# AMBROSIA FREEZE

1 (8-ounce) container strawberry cream cheese

2 medium bananas, mashed

1 (14-ounce) can **EAGLE BRAND®** Sweetened Condensed Milk (NOT evaporated milk)

1 (8-ounce) container low-fat strawberry yogurt

2 tablespoons lemon juice

1 (11-ounce) can mandarin orange sections, drained

1 (8-ounce) can crushed pineapple, well drained

½ cup toasted flaked coconut

Red food coloring (optional)

**1.** In large bowl with electric mixer on low speed, beat cream cheese and bananas until smooth. Beat in **EAGLE BRAND®**, yogurt and lemon juice until blended. Stir in orange sections, pineapple and coconut. Stir in food coloring (optional). Spoon into ungreased 11×7-inch baking dish.

**2.** Cover and freeze 6 hours or until firm. Remove from freezer 15 minutes before serving. Cut into 1×1-inch cubes; serve in stemmed glasses or dessert dishes. Store leftovers covered in freezer.

# Peppermint Ice Cream Gems

*Makes 2 dozen gems*

3 cups finely crushed crème-filled chocolate sandwich cookies (about 36 cookies)

½ cup (1 stick) butter or margarine, melted

1 (14-ounce) can **EAGLE BRAND®** Sweetened Condensed Milk (NOT evaporated milk)

¼ cup white crème de menthe liqueur or ½ teaspoon peppermint extract

2 tablespoons peppermint schnapps

1 to 2 drops red or green food coloring (optional)

2 cups (1 pint) whipping cream, whipped (NOT nondairy whipped topping)

**1.** In medium bowl, combine cookie crumbs and butter. Press 2 rounded tablespoons crumb mixture each on bottom and up sides of 24 standard (2½-inch) paper-lined muffin cups.

**2.** In large bowl, combine **EAGLE BRAND®**, crème de menthe, schnapps and food coloring (optional). Fold in whipped cream. Spoon mixture into crusts.

**3.** Freeze 6 hours or until firm. To serve, remove paper liners. Garnish as desired. Store leftovers covered in freezer.

# FRENCH APPLE BREAD PUDDING

*Makes 6 to 9 servings*

| | |
|---|---|
| 4 cups cubed French bread | 1¾ cups hot water |
| ½ cup raisins (optional) | ¼ cup (½ stick) butter or margarine, melted |
| 3 eggs | |
| 1 (14-ounce) can **EAGLE BRAND®** Sweetened Condensed Milk (NOT evaporated milk) | 1 teaspoon ground cinnamon |
| | 1 teaspoon vanilla extract |
| 3 medium apples, peeled, cored and finely chopped | Ice cream (optional) |

**1.** Preheat oven to 350°F. Combine bread cubes and raisins (optional) in buttered 9-inch square pan.

**2.** In large bowl, beat eggs. Add **EAGLE BRAND®**, apples, water, butter, cinnamon and vanilla. Pour evenly over bread cubes, moistening completely.

**3.** Bake 50 to 55 minutes or until knife inserted near center comes out clean. Cool slightly. Serve warm with ice cream (optional). Store leftovers covered in refrigerator.

# CREAMY BANANA PUDDING

*Makes 8 to 10 servings*

1 (14-ounce) can **EAGLE BRAND®** Sweetened Condensed Milk (NOT evaporated milk)

1½ cups cold water

1 (4-serving size) package instant vanilla pudding and pie filling mix

2 cups (1 pint) whipping cream, whipped

36 vanilla wafers

3 medium bananas, sliced and dipped in lemon juice

**1.** In large bowl, combine **EAGLE BRAND®** and water. Add pudding mix; beat until well blended. Chill 5 minutes.

**2.** Fold in whipped cream. Spoon 1 cup pudding mixture into 2½-quart glass serving bowl or divide among 8 to 10 individual serving dishes.

**3.** Top with one-third each vanilla wafers, bananas and pudding mixture. Repeat layers twice, ending with pudding mixture. Chill. Garnish as desired. Store leftovers covered in refrigerator.

# CRUNCHY PEPPERMINT CANDY ICE CREAM

*Makes 1½ quarts*

- 2 cups (1 pint) light cream
- 1 (14-ounce) can **EAGLE BRAND®** Sweetened Condensed Milk (NOT evaporated milk)
- 1¼ cups water
- ½ cup crushed hard peppermint candy
- 1 tablespoon vanilla extract
- Additional crushed hard peppermint candy (optional)

**1.** In ice cream freezer container, combine cream, **EAGLE BRAND®**, water, peppermint candy and vanilla. Freeze according to manufacturer's instructions.

**2.** Garnish with additional crushed peppermint candy (optional). Store leftovers covered in freezer.

# Chocolate Peanut Butter Dessert Sauce

*Makes about 1½ cups sauce*

2 (1-ounce) squares semisweet chocolate, chopped

2 tablespoons creamy peanut butter

1 (14-ounce) can **EAGLE BRAND**® Sweetened Condensed Milk (NOT evaporated milk)

2 tablespoons milk

1 teaspoon vanilla extract

Fresh fruit, ice cream or cake

**1.** In medium saucepan over medium-low heat, melt chocolate and peanut butter with **EAGLE BRAND**® and milk, stirring constantly. Remove from heat; stir in vanilla. Cool slightly.

**2.** Serve warm as fruit dipping sauce, or over ice cream or cake. Store leftovers covered in refrigerator.

# CHERRY CORDIAL ICE CREAM

2 cups (1 pint) half-and-half

2 cups (1 pint) whipping cream

1 (14-ounce) can **EAGLE BRAND®** Sweetened Condensed Milk (NOT evaporated milk)

1 (10-ounce) jar maraschino cherries (without stems), well drained and chopped (about 1 cup)

¾ cup miniature semisweet chocolate chips

1 tablespoon vanilla extract

½ teaspoon almond extract

In ice cream freezer container, combine all ingredients; mix well. Freeze according to manufacturer's instructions. Store leftovers covered in freezer.

**Refrigerator-freezer method:** Omit half-and-half. Whip whipping cream. In large bowl, combine **EAGLE BRAND®**, ½ cup chopped maraschino cherries, ½ cup miniature chocolate chips, 2 teaspoons vanilla and ¼ teaspoon almond extract; mix well. Fold in whipped cream. Pour into 9×5-inch loaf pan or other 2-quart container. Cover. Freeze 6 hours or until firm. Freeze leftovers.

# CHOCOLATE ICE CREAM CUPS

2 cups (12 ounces) semisweet
   chocolate chips

1 (14-ounce) can **EAGLE BRAND®**
   Sweetened Condensed Milk
   (NOT evaporated milk)

1 cup finely ground pecans
   Ice cream, any flavor

**1.** In large heavy saucepan over low heat, melt chocolate chips with **EAGLE BRAND®**; remove from heat. Stir in pecans. In individual paper-lined muffin cups, pour about 2 tablespoons chocolate mixture. With lightly greased spoon, spread chocolate on bottom and up side of each cup.

**2.** Freeze 2 hours or until firm. Before serving, remove paper liners. Fill chocolate cups with ice cream. Store unfilled cups tightly covered in freezer.

> **Note:** It is easier to remove the paper liners if the chocolate cups sit at room temperature for about 5 minutes first.

# INDEX

**Nuts**